THE SPIRIT OF
THE WALDORF SCHOOL

[V]

FOUNDATIONS OF WALDORF EDUCATION

RUDOLF STEINER

THE SPIRIT
OF THE
WALDORF
SCHOOL

Lectures Surrounding the Founding
of the First Waldorf School
Stuttgart–1919
and
An Essay from *The Social Future*
February 1920

Translated by
Robert F. Lathe and Nancy Parsons Whittaker

Anthroposophic Press

The publisher wishes to acknowledge the inspiration
and support of Connie and Robert Dulaney

❖ ❖ ❖

This book is a translation of *Die Waldorfschule und ihr Geist* (volume 297
in the Collected Works) and "Die pädagogische Zielsetzung der Waldorfschule
in Stuttgart," from *Soziale Zukunft,* February 1920 (found in volume 24
in the Collected Works), both published by Rudolf Steiner Verlag,
Dornach, Switzerland, 1980 and 1982, respectively.

© Copyright Anthroposophic Press, 1995

Published in the United States by Anthroposophic Press
3390 Route 9, Hudson, NY 12534

10 9 8 7 6 5 4 3 2

Printed in the United States of America

Contents

LECTURE ONE

The Intent of the Waldorf School

Freeing the schools of politics and economics. The art of education provides a means to use subject matter to develop strength of soul. Thinking, Feeling and Willing from the point of view of life before birth and after death. The inner relationship of the teacher to the child requires complete freedom in education. Kretzschmar as an example of this longing.

LECTURE TWO

The Spirit of the Waldorf School

Guiding principles for education result from an anthroposophical study of humanity. Examples of child developmental stages and the form of the curriculum. The child must be guided to learn from life.

LECTURE SIX

Spiritual Science and Pedagogy

Limits of scientific method. Children as imitative beings. The child's devotion to true authority. Educating the whole person. Child's developing capacity for judgment. Goal of spiritual science to add to existing culture, not to replace culture.

The Pedagogical Objective
of the Waldorf School in Stuttgart

An essay by Rudolf Steiner from the journal *The Social Future*

Translators' Note

OUR EXPERIENCE IS THAT a vivid, imaginative relationship with Rudolf Steiner the man is more possible through his lectures than through his more formal written works. Whether we read the original German or an English translation (good *or* bad), the living quality of the moment of delivery emerges from the printed page, and, instead of reading a transcript, we find ourselves listening to a man filled with warmth for his audience, enthusiasm for his task and a clear sense of the urgency, even the desperation, of modern times. Our goal has been to render a translation that makes this living experience of a lecture hall in 1919 accessible to as many people as possible. The guiding question we have held before us throughout this work is, "How would Rudolf Steiner have spoken this thought to an American audience in 1994?" To this end, we have passed these lectures through the filter of multiple oral readings in an attempt not only to obtain a flowing presentation, but to find words that would ring true to the American ear as well as to the American eye.

These lectures can, of course, be read silently to oneself without compromising the truths they hold. However, we suggest that a more enriching experience may be possible by reading them out loud. Our hope is that you will at least try this approach, and that, doing so, you will find yourself in a crowded lecture hall, listening to a man of profoundly uncommon insight address the heart of our social illnesses and point the way to a human future.

We have been greatly assisted in our efforts by the valuable work of Will Marsh and Judith Sweningsen, our copyeditors at Anthroposophic Press, whose many useful suggestions have made the text clearer and more direct. For this, we are very grateful.

Introduction

Robert F. Lathe and Nancy Parsons Whittaker

BY THE SPRING OF 1919, nothing was left of what had been called Germany and little remained of what had been Europe. The dissolution of society had gone far beyond the fall of governments, beyond the collapse of institutions, beyond the blurring of social conventions and mores, beyond harsh economic reality. This destruction bored into the heart and mind of each individual who walked the streets of a devastated world. Despair replaced hope. Shame slouched where pride once strode. Knowledge dissolved into confusion. What had seemed a wellspring of ideas was revealed as only cracked, barren earth. Everywhere lay the rubble of old foundations.

The German people believed that its Imperial structure, erected half a century ago, would last for an unlimited time. In August 1914, they felt that the immanent catastrophe of war would prove this structure invincible. Today, only its ruins are left. After such an experience, retrospection is in order, for this experience has proved the opinions of half a century, especially the dominant thoughts of the war years, to be tragically erroneous.[1]

From all directions came not retrospection, but the struggle for control. In large and small ways, thousands of people

---

1. Rudolf Steiner, "Call to the German People and the Civilized World," March 1919, in *Towards Social Renewal: Basic Issues of the Social Question*, Rudolf Steiner Press, London, 1977. Trans. by Frank Thomas Smith.

engaged in an effort to replace the crumbled order with a better world. The solutions tended in opposing directions and ranged from military dictatorship to the creation of a "soviet" in Bavaria. Ideology, not ideas, became the driving force of social activity. These polar efforts tore at the shreds of Germany. The rancor of opposing opinions succeeded in claiming public attention for a struggle that could hold no hope, regardless of the outcome. Behind the din of diverging forces, human beings cried out for a better society, but the clamor was so loud it was all but impossible to hear a thoughtful response. In July 1917, Rudolf Steiner had presented the German and Austrian governments with a proposal detailing how the principles of the Threefold Social Organism could be realized. Within days after it reached the German palace, internal political turmoil rendered any consideration of his ideas impossible. The Austrian government likewise failed to respond. Steiner turned to the German people. In public lectures he pointed again and again to the need to go beyond slogans and empty phrases, to fearlessly evaluate the past and face the future with clear commitment. His "Call to the German People and the Civilized World" was a deeply considered plea for a new direction based upon an unflinching evaluation of the past and a deep understanding of human needs. These efforts notwithstanding, Steiner soon realized that his ideas alone were insufficient to move a society forward.

Rudolf Steiner was forced to ask why it was that no one seemed to be able to hear what could be done to form a truly new society, a truly human society. He concluded that no one could hear him because the education people had been given left them unable to consider, and therefore unable to work with, anything not based in familiar routine. A window of opportunity for social change was open. Germany was in a state of chaos and the German people were searching for an answer to the question of how to reorganize society. The question was, how could a positive change be effected? The needed social change could result from neither political coercion nor revolutionary upheaval. A truly human society can be the outcome only of the fully developed human capacities of Thinking, Feeling and Willing. When Thinking is developed, it becomes possible to clearly perceive present circumstances and form accurate imaginations of positive change. Rightly developed Feeling enables people to sense how to unite these imaginations with the outer world. A developed Will grants the possibility of transforming these imaginations into deeds for the world. Only in this way can a sound human society develop. Rudolf Steiner concluded that truly human social change would not be possible until a sufficient number of people had received an education that undertook to develop complete human beings.

Emil Molt, Director of the Waldorf-Astoria Cigarette Company and student of Rudolf Steiner, first had the desire to be active in a reformation of German society during a lecture given by Dr. Steiner in Switzerland in early November 1918. Shortly thereafter, during a mid-November discussion with some of the workers at the Waldorf-Astoria factory, he resolved to create a school, though the school as yet had no firm form. In a discussion with Rudolf Steiner in January 1919, the latter mentioned that in order to achieve a real social reformation, schools must be formed.

Three months later, following a lecture by Steiner to the factory workers,[2] the workers expressed a desire for a new school, a desire which was, of course, immediately taken up by Molt. Some weeks before, Molt had already begun discussions with

---

2. Rudolf Steiner, "Proletarische Forderungen und deren künftige praktische Verwiklichung" [Proletarian demands and their future practical realization], contained in *Neugestaltung des sozialen Organismus* [Reorganization of the social organism], Rudolf Steiner Verlag, Dornach Switzerland, 1983. (GA 330, 4/23/19).

the Minister of Education concerning the formation of a new
unified school, discussions that were tending in a positive
direction. Two days after the meeting with the factory workers,
a first "teachers" meeting took place with Steiner, Molt and two
of the future Waldorf School teachers (Stockmeyer and Hahn).
Three weeks later, the Minister of Education agreed to the new
school. In particular, it was agreed that the new school would
meet the standards set for public school students at the end of
the third, sixth and eighth grades. However, during these three
periods, what and how the students were to be taught were left
to the pedagogical leadership of the school. This agreement
allowed Rudolf Steiner, Emil Molt and others to begin the formation of the Waldorf School.

The following weeks were filled with activity. Teachers needed
to be found. Buildings needed to be located and renovated. The
seminar for teachers was held. Finally, the Free Waldorf School
opened amid great festivities on September 7, 1919.

The Free Waldorf School was founded upon the impulse for
social change, upon the need to reform society into a community which takes into account the true Being of Humanity. Into
the desire for reform were sown the life-giving forces of the
teachers' inner work and Rudolf Steiner's spiritual insight. The
goal of this education was that, through living inner work
guided by the insights of Rudolf Steiner, the teachers would
develop in the children such power of thought, such depth of
feeling, such strength of will that they would emerge from their
school years as full members of the Human Community, able
to meet and transform the world.

These six lectures and one essay are an exciting presentation
of the heart of this education. The first two lectures introduce
the goals and foundations of the Free Waldorf School.
Throughout these lectures, Rudolf Steiner clearly outlines in
simple, straightforward language filled with enthusiasm and

hope for the future, the social impulse, the foundation of inner work, and the intent to graduate young men and women able to powerfully "put themselves into life." We find it quite significant that despite the increasing breadth of the successive audiences, Rudolf Steiner's presentation of the role of spiritual science as fundamental to the renewal of education remains uncompromised. From six different perspectives, the heart of this education shines forth. These lectures reveal the ground on which all else in Waldorf education must stand and the necessary path to walk. It is our hope that they will become a starting point for those making first inquiries about Waldorf Education and Anthroposophy as well as a fundamental resource for those already involved in this work.

THE SPIRIT OF
THE WALDORF SCHOOL

Foreword to the First Three Lectures [1]

Herbert Hahn

FOR ALL THOSE WHO STOOD at Rudolf Steiner's side, the time in which the following lectures were given is unforgettable. The general collapse in Central Europe which ended the World War largely dissolved the apparently solid government and social structure. Search high and low, it was impossible to find relevant ideas that could help master the ensuing chaotic situation. This serious hour of world history posed but one question; however, the people called upon to answer it, failed.

Then Rudolf Steiner published his "Call to the German People and the Civilized World." Through clear, concise, penetrating formulations he showed that, seen from the point of view of world history, the political and social structure that had just collapsed had actually been ruined by its own lack of ideas. Out of his insight into Spiritual Reality, Rudolf Steiner brought the impulse of the Threefold Social Organism into the context of world history as the fundamental, organizational and constructive principle needed not only for Central Europe, but also for the whole civilized world. The Threefold Social Organism reflects the need for: 1) a politically free cultural life,

---

1. Translated from Rudolf Steiner, *Die Waldorfschule und ihr Geist. Welche Gesichtspunkte liegen der Errichtung der Waldorfschule Zugrunde,* lectures of August 24 and 31, Rudolf Steiner Verlag, Dornach, 1980.

self-administered and self-sustaining, 2) an economic life based upon the fraternal-associative principle, free of national and international political influence, and, 3) a strongly self-limiting government that could rejuvenate and reform itself according to the consciousness of the time. Whenever Rudolf Steiner spoke of these great needs, he emphasized that they were not formulated simply out of clever personal consideration. The objective necessity of the times induced the birth of the Threefold Social Organism which contains the social ideas that could counteract the chaos that otherwise threatens to increase.

The young social impulse was taken up with particular enthusiasm in southern Germany. Stuttgart became a center for the Threefold Social Organism Movement. People were burning to form new initiatives. Workers from all walks of life met, banded together and took part in Rudolf Steiner's lectures in overcrowded, smoke-filled rooms. Captivated by his words, people beheld the power of the Conscience of the Times. They were happy to find a man who did not talk like someone living in an ivory tower. They talked with him about the great social problems in very concrete detail, literally night after night into the wee hours of the morning.

In those days and in such discussions, thoughts of an all-encompassing pedagogical reformation also arose. These soon crystallized into the core of the Threefold work. People felt that only a social pedagogy held within a free Spiritual Life could bring life-giving water into other areas of a parched and barren society. On the crest of the great wave of the Threefold Movement, Emil Molt, then the Director of the Waldorf-Astoria Factory in Stuttgart, put this impulse into effect by founding a school. Thus, it came about that in August of 1919, Rudolf Steiner gave the course on the general study of the human being, mentioned in these lectures, for the soon-to-be faculty of the new school, the Free Waldorf School in

Stuttgart. Everything else in these lectures must also be seen from this perspective.

The lectures can be understood only by those who attempt to form a picture of the deep-seated seriousness of the times, who, through creative imagination, place themselves within this enormous activity, within the fire of a new social will that stands behind each word.

For Rudolf Steiner himself, what was important was that people hear what was really decisive, in spite of coincidentally similar words, in spite of similar-sounding sentences, in spite of similar abstract thoughts. He did not see the renewal of pedagogy as one social reform among many. He saw it as *the* source of social renewal for the coming generations of young people.

. . . .

HERBERT HAHN was born May 5, 1890, in Pernau, and died June 20, 1970, in Stuttgart. At the close of the First World War, he was very active in Rudolf Steiner's Movement for the Threefolding of the Social Organism. Immediately following the War, Hahn was chosen by Emil Molt to coordinate the activities of the Waldorf Astoria Cigarette Factory's adult education program. In 1919, he joined with Molt, Steiner and E. A. K. Stockmeyer (another teacher) in the conversations with the Minister of Education leading to the founding of the first Free Waldorf School. Hahn attended the original seminar for the faculty and began teaching French in the lower grades when the Waldorf School opened. Subsequently, he taught social science and was later given the task of presenting the Free Religion lessons. Out of his experience he delivered a series of lectures on religious education for children at the Christian Community Priest's Seminary in Stuttgart. These were later published in English under the title, *From the Wellsprings of the Soul*. From 1931–39, Hahn taught in Holland in the Hague. Following the Second World War, Hahn again taught in Stuttgart, where he wrote his great work, *Vom Genius Europas* [The genius of Europe]. Toward the end of his life, Hahn returned to the question of "free religious instruction" and was instrumental in its renewal in Waldorf education in Germany. Herbert Hahn was also the author of *Der Weg der mich führte—Lebenserrinerungen* [The way that led me—reminiscences] and *Rudolf Steiner, Wie Ich ihn sah und erlebte* [Rudolf Steiner, as I saw and experienced him].

1

The Intent of the Waldorf School

TODAY I would like to speak to you about the Waldorf School, founded by our friend Mr. Molt. You well know, from the announcements distributed about this school, that our intention is to take a first step along the path we would want the cultural life of the Threefold Social Organism to take. In establishing the Waldorf School, Mr. Molt has, to a large extent, felt motivated to do something to further the development of inner spirituality. He hopes to do something that will point the way for the present and future social tasks of the Threefold Social Organism. Obviously, the Waldorf School can be successful only if it is completely inspired by the Spirit that aspires toward the threefold nature of the social organism. It is easy to comprehend that such a first step cannot immediately be perfect. And along with this insight, belongs an understanding. We would so very much like to see this understanding offered to the founding of this school, at least from a limited group for the present. The work needed for the Waldorf School has already begun. It has begun with those who have offered to help and whom we have taken under consideration to contribute pedagogically to the Waldorf School. They are now attending a recently begun seminar in preparation for the work there. Gathered in this seminar are only those who, as a result of their talents and bearing, appear capable of working in the cultural movement which the Waldorf School should serve. Of course, they appear particularly called to work in the pedagogical area. Nevertheless, the Waldorf School must be offered understanding, at least from a small group for the present. You will notice more and more as you become aware of social reality that the mutual understanding of people regarding their work will be a major factor in the social life of the future. So, it seems to me that those persons who have themselves shown interest are most suitable to participate in the discussions, to be held here today and next Sunday, concerning the efforts of the Waldorf School.

Indeed, it seems to be of the utmost importance that something more comes about to encourage this understanding. Unquestionably, all parents who want their children to attend the Waldorf School have a broad interest in what this school should achieve. It appears to me to be a particular need that, before the opening of the Waldorf School in the first half of September, we meet again, along with all the parents who want their children to attend. Only what is rooted in the understanding of those involved in such initiatives with their souls and with their whole lives can flourish in a truly socially oriented social life.

Today I would like to speak with you about the goals of the Waldorf School and, to some extent, the desired instructional methods. With the Waldorf School we hope to create something that, in our judgment, needs to be based upon the particular historical stage of human development of the present and near future. You should not misunderstand the establishment of the Waldorf School by believing that everything in the old school system is bad. Nor should you believe that our starting point for the establishment of the Waldorf School is simply a criticism of the old school system. It is actually quite a different question.

In the course of the last three to four centuries a social life has been formed: a state/rights life, a spiritual/cultural life, an economic life, which have assumed a certain configuration. This social life, particularly the educational system, "resists," we might say, the renewal of our social relationships, as I have recently so often argued. In the last three to four centuries the educational system has become so completely dependent upon the state that we could say that it is, in a quite peculiar way, a part of the state. Now, we can say that to a certain extent—however, only to a very limited extent—the educational institutions to which people have become accustomed were at one time appropriate to the configuration of the states of the civilized world. But what we strive for here is a *transformation* of the present social configuration. The understanding that is to form the basis of future social life requires that the system of education not remain in the same relationship to the state that it has had until now. For if we strive for a social form of economic life, the need to remove cultural life from the influence of politics and economics will be all the more urgent. This applies in particular to the administration of the educational system. People have felt this need for a very long time. But all pedagogical aspirations in the most recent past, and particularly at present, have something oppressive about them, something that hardly considers the general point of view of cultural life. This has all come about through the peculiar way in which government officials in the most recent past, and especially at present, have publicly addressed such pedagogical aspirations.

Naturally, the Waldorf School will have to reconcile itself with current institutions and public opinion concerning education and teaching. We will not immediately be able to achieve all that we wish to achieve—quite understandably we will, on the whole, find it necessary to comply with the present requirements of public education. We will find it necessary that the graduates of our school reach the level demanded for transfer to institutions of higher education, in particular, the universities. We will, therefore, be unable to organize our educational material so that it represents what we find to be the ideal of a truly humane education. In a manner of speaking, we will be able to use only the holes that still remain in the tightly woven web that spreads over the educational system. In these holes we will work to instruct the children entrusted to the Waldorf School, in the sense of a completely free cultural life. We plan to take full advantage of every opportunity presented. We most certainly will not be able to create a model school. However, we can show to what degree inner strengthening and a truly inner education of the child is possible, when it is achieved solely out of the needs of the cultural life, and not through something imposed from outside.

We will have to struggle against much resistance, particularly regarding the understanding that people can offer us today. We will have much resistance to overcome, precisely because, regarding present-day understanding, as I have often mentioned here, people just pass each other by. Yet, we repeatedly experience, precisely in the area of education, that people elsewhere also speak about a transformation of the educational system from the same point of view as represented here. The people who are involved at present with the latest principles of education listen and say, "Yes, that is exactly right, that is what we wanted all along!" In reality, they want something completely different. But today we are so far removed from the subjects about which we speak, that we listen and believe we mean the same things with the same words, when, in actuality, we mean just the opposite.

The power of the empty phrase has had a prolonged reign and has become very strong in our civilized world. Haven't we experienced this in the greatest measure? And into this reign of the empty phrase has been woven the most terrible event that has occurred in world history—the horrible catastrophe of the war in the past years! Just think about how closely the empty phrase is connected with this catastrophe! Think about the role it has played, and you will arrive at a truly dismaying judgment about the reign of the empty phrase in our time.

So today, in the pedagogical area also, we hear, "What is important is not the subject matter, but the pupil," from those who strive for something quite different from what we intend.

You know that since we have no choice but to use the words in our vocabulary, we too will often have to say, "The important thing in education is not the subject matter, but the pupil." We want to use the subject matter in our Waldorf School in such a way that at each stage of instruction it will serve to improve the human development of the pupil regarding the formation of the will, feeling and intellect, rather than serving to provide superficial knowledge. We should not offer each subject for the sole purpose of imparting knowledge. The teaching of a subject should become an art in the hands of the teachers. The way we treat a subject should enable the children to grow into life and fill their proper place. We must become aware that each stage of human life brings forth out of the depths of human nature the tendency toward particular powers of the soul. If we do not educate these inclinations at the relevant age, they cannot, in truth, be educated later. They become stunted, and render people unable to meet the demands of life connected with will, connected with feeling, connected with intellect. People cannot rightly take up the position into which life places them. Between the change of teeth and sexual maturity, that is, in the period of real education, it is particularly important to recognize the powers of soul and body that children need to develop in order to later fulfill their places in life.

Someone who has absorbed the pedagogical thoughts of the last decades could hear everything that I have now said, and say, "Exactly my opinion!" But what he or she does pedagogically on the basis of this opinion is not at all what we desire here. In the present, we commonly speak past each other, and thus we must, in a somewhat deeper way, attempt to draw attention to the real intention of the Waldorf School.

Above all, people are obsessed, we could almost say, with the need to take everything absolutely. By that I mean the following: If we speak today about how people should be educated in this or that way (we only want to speak about education; but we could, in various ways, extend the same considerations to other areas of life), we always think that education should concern something that is absolutely valid for humanity. We think it must be something that, so to speak, is absolutely right, something that, if it had only been available, would have been used, for example, for the people in Ancient Egypt or in Ancient Greece. It must also be useful in four thousand years for the people who will live then. It must also be useful in China, Japan, and so forth. This obsession of modern people, that they can set up something absolutely valid, is the greatest enemy of all Reality. Thus we should keep in mind, we should recognize, that we are not people in an absolute sense, but people of a quite particular age. We should recognize that people of the present age are, in their soul and physical body, constituted differently from, for example, the Greeks and Romans. Modern people are also constituted differently from the way in which people will be constituted in a relatively short time, in five hundred years. Thus, we do not understand the task of education in an absolute sense. Rather, we understand it as emerging from the needs of human culture in the present and near future.

We ask how civilized human beings are constituted today and base our viewpoint concerning methods of education upon that. We know quite well that a Greek or Roman had to have been raised differently, and, also, that people will have to be raised differently again in five hundred years. We want to create a basis of upbringing for our present time and the near future. We can really dedicate ourselves to humanity only if we become aware of these real conditions for human development and do not always keep nebulous goals in mind. Thus, it is necessary to point out what threatens human development, especially in connection with the educational instruction of the present, and what, in the present time, we want to avoid.

I have just pointed out that some people say, "The subject matter is not important, the pupil is important. The way the teacher acts in instructing the pupil is important. The way the subject matter is used for teaching, for educating, is important." At the same time, however, we see a remarkably different direction in the very people who say this. We see a tendency that, to some extent, thoroughly paralyses and negates their demand of "more for the pupil than for the subject matter."

People who say such things perceive that, as a result of specialization, science has gradually moved beyond normal intellectual comprehension. They see it taught in a superficial way, purely for the sake of knowledge, without any attention to the pupil. So now people say, "You may not do that. You must educate the pupil according to the nature of young people." But how can we learn how the pupil needs to be treated? People expect to learn this from the very science that was formed under the regime they want to fight! They want to know the nature of the child, but they employ all kinds of experimental psychologies, those methods science developed by forcing itself into the very situation people desire to remedy. So, following the path of experimental psychology, they want to conduct research at the universities to determine which special methods are right for pedagogy. They want to carry experimental pedagogy into university life, to carry in all the one-sidedness that science has assumed. Yes, people want to reform! People want to reform because they have a vague feeling that reform is necessary. But this feeling arises out of the very spirit that has brought about the old methods they now want to keep. People would like to found an educational science, but they want to base it upon that scientific spirit that has arisen because people were not brought up correctly.

People still do not see the very strong forces at work in the development of our culture. People do not at all see that even though they have the best intentions they become involved in such conflicts and contradictions. Although some people may have another view about this, we can nevertheless say that Johann Friedrich Herbart is in many ways one of the most significant people in the pedagogical field. Herbart's pedagogical writing and work place him in a position very unusual in recent times. His book, *Allgemeine Pädagogik* [Pedagogical theory], appeared in 1806, and he continued to learn through his own pedagogical work after that. The 1835 *Survey* of his pedagogical lectures shows how he advanced in his understanding of pedagogical problems. We can say that a good portion of the pedagogical development in the second half of the nineteenth century stemmed from the impulse of Herbart's pedagogy, since, for example, the whole Austrian educational system has been inspired by it. In Germany, too, a great deal of the spirit of Herbart's pedagogy still lives today in views on education. Thus today, if we want to orient ourselves to the idea that we live in a particular cultural age, we must confront the content of Herbart's pedagogy, and discover what a pedagogical force, a pedagogical reality, actually is.

To properly understand Herbart, we can say that all his thoughts and ideas stand fully within that cultural period that, for the true observer of human development, clearly ended in the mid-fifteenth century. Since the middle of the fifteenth century, we stand in a new epoch of human civilization. But, we have not followed the impulses that bloomed in the fifteenth century and have, therefore, achieved little; and what was active before the fifteenth century continues in our lives. It has brilliantly, significantly, continued in our pedagogical life in all that Herbart worked out and all that he inspired. Human development during the long period that began in the eighth century B.C. and ended in the middle of the fifteenth century A.D. can be characterized by saying that intellect and feeling were instinctive. Since the middle of the fifteenth century, humanity has striven toward a consciousness of personality and toward putting itself in charge of its own personality. For the present and future, the most important change in the historical impulse of human development is the decline of instinctive understanding. No change is more important than the decline of the instinctive soul activity of the Greco-Roman age, and the beginning of the new epoch in the fifteenth century! The particular considerations which prove what I have just said are presented in my writings and publications. Here we must accept as a fact that as of the middle of the fifteenth century, something new began for humanity, namely the aspiration toward conscious personal activity, where previously an instinctive understanding and soul activity were present. This instinctive understanding and soul activity had a certain tendency to cultivate intellectual life one-sidedly. It could seem strange to say that the time in which understanding was instinctively oriented led to a peak of a certain kind of education, an overdevelopment of human intellectuality. But you will not be amazed by such an idea if you consider that what affects a person intellectually need not always be something consciously personal, that instinctive intelligence in particular can come to the highest degree of expression. You need only remember that people discovered paper much later than wasps did through their instinctive intelligence, for wasp nests are made of paper, just as people, with their intelligence, make paper. Intellect need not affect only people. It can also permeate other beings without necessarily simultaneously bringing the personality, which should develop only just now in our age, to its highest level.

Now obviously, in a period in which intelligence endeavored to develop itself to its highest level, the desire was also present to permeate the educational system, and everything that the educational system permeates, with the intellect. Those who now examine Herbart's pedagogy find that it emphasizes that the will and feeling should be educated. However, if you do not simply remain with the words, but if you go on to Reality, you will notice something. You will notice that an education based upon discipline and order, as is Herbart's pedagogy, desperately requires something. It should educate the will, it should educate the feeling. However, what Herbart offers in content is, in truth, suited only to educating the intellect. What he offers as pedagogical principles is instinctively felt, most particularly by Herbart himself, to be insufficient to comprehend the whole human; it comprehends only the human as an intellectual being. Thus, out of a healthy instinct he demands over and over again that there must also be an education of the feeling and will.

The question is, can we, with this as a foundation, really teach and educate the feeling and will in an appropriate way, in a way befitting human nature? I would like to point out that Herbart assumes that all pedagogy must be based upon psychology and philosophy, that is, upon the general world conception and understanding of the human soul life. Herbart's thinking is thoroughly oriented to the abstract, and he has carried this abstract thinking into his psychology. I would like to examine Herbart's psychology with you by means of a simplified example.

We know that in human nature three basic forces are at work: Thinking, Feeling and Willing. We know that the health of the human soul depends upon the appropriate development of these three basic forces, upon each of these basic forces coming into its own. What in Herbart's philosophy develops these basic forces? Herbart is really of the opinion that the entire soul life first opens in the conceptual life—feeling is only a conceptual form for him, as is willing, endeavoring, desiring. So you hear from Herbart's followers, "If we try to drink water because we are thirsty, we do not actually desire the real substance of the water. Rather, we try to rid ourselves of the idea that thirst causes in us and to replace it in our soul with the idea of a quenched thirst. Thus, we do not desire the water at all. Instead, we desire that the idea of thirst cease and be replaced with the idea of quenched thirst. If we desire a lively conversation, we do not actually desire the content of this conversation. Rather, we long for a change in our present ideas and are really trying to obtain the idea that will occur through a lively conversation. If we have a desire, we do not have it as a result of basic forces at work in our soul. Rather, we have the desire because a particularly pleasant idea easily arises in our consciousness and easily overcomes the opposing inhibitions. This experience is desire. The ideas cause everything. Everything else is, in truth, only what the activity of the ideas reveals." We can say that the whole Herbartian way of thinking, and everything which has been built upon it—and more than you think has been based upon the Herbartian way of thinking—is permeated by an unconscious belief that the true life of the soul takes place in the struggle between restraint and support of ideas. In this way of thinking, what appear to be feeling and willing exist only as emotions of the life of ideas. We should not be confused that many modern people who are concerned with pedagogy oppose teaching and bringing up children in this way, and yet direct their efforts only toward the life of ideas. They say they oppose it, of course, but they do not act accordingly; they base everything they do on the thought, "Conceptual ideas are what matter!" The strangest thing we can experience today is the lives of people caught in such contradictions. People preach and lecture today that we should indeed look at the whole person, that we should be careful not to neglect the soul life, the life of feeling and willing! Yet, if we return to what is practiced, precisely those who talk so much about the development of feeling and willing are the ones who intellectualize teaching and education. These people do not understand even themselves because what they say is so far from the subject and has become just empty phrases.

We must look at these things intensely when we try to meet the demands of our cultural period, particularly regarding teaching and education.

So, I now come to the main point! People say that the subject matter does not matter so much as the pupil. But, as I have already mentioned, they want to study the pupil with a science of education that uses the methods of an imbalanced science. However, they do not even come close through the superficially oriented science of the last centuries. They need a very different orientation to understand humans. This other orientation is sought by our Anthroposophically oriented spiritual science. We want to replace the superficial anthropology, the superficial understanding of humanity, with something that studies the whole person, the physical, emotional and mental essence. Certainly, today people emphasize, even literally, the mental and the emotional, but they do not understand it. People do not pay any attention at all to the fact that something like the Herbartian philosophy, particularly as it regards the soul, is quite intellectually based, and therefore, cannot be integrated into our cultural period. On the other hand, Herbart wants to base his work on philosophy. But that philosophy upon which he builds likewise ended with the period that concluded in the middle of the fifteenth century. In our time, a philosophy founded in spirituality needs to have room. Out of this new philosophy, the soul and spirit can be so strengthened that we can link them to what we learn through anthropology regarding the physical aspects of humans. For in our time, the knowledge concerning the physical aspects of humans is truly great, even though it barely mentions the soul.

If you look at modern psychology with healthy common sense, you have to ask what you could really gain from it. There you will find disputes about the world of thinking, the world of feeling, the world of willing. But what you will find about these words, "thinking, feeling, willing," is only word play. You will not become any wiser concerning the nature of thinking, feeling and willing if you search through modern psychology. Thus you cannot base a genuinely good pedagogy upon modern psychology. First, you must go into what is pertinent about the true nature of thinking, feeling and willing. To do that, the outdated scholastic spirit so prevalent in modern psychology is not necessary; what is necessary is a real gift for observing human life. What we observe today in psychology and in pedagogical laboratories appears to be efforts carried by the best of intentions. These efforts have nonetheless taken the direction they have taken because, fundamentally, the ability to pursue a true observation of people is lacking. Today most of all, people would like to put the developing child in a psychological laboratory and superficially study inner development, because they have lost the living relationship between people. A living way of observing is necessary for life, and it has largely been lost.

Today people talk about the spirit and soul in much the way that they speak about external characteristics. If we meet a child, a person of thirty-five and an old person, we say, "This is a person, this is a person, this is a person." Although the abstract idea of "a person" is often useful, a real observation distinguishes a reality in the end, namely, that the child will become a person of thirty-five years and that a person of thirty-five will become old. True observation must be quite clear concerning the difference in this development. Now, it is relatively easy to distinguish a child from a person of thirty-five and from an elderly person. However, a true observation of such differences concerning the inner aspects of people is somewhat more difficult. Thus, in the present, we often become entangled in questions of unity and multiplicity that arise, for example, from the three aspects of the soul life. Are thinking, feeling and willing completely separate things? If they are, then our soul life would be absolutely divided into three parts. There would be no transition between willing, feeling and thinking, and, therefore, human intellect, and we could simply delineate, as modern people do so easily, these aspects of human soul life. For the very reason that we cannot do that, Herbart tries to treat thinking, feeling and willing uniformly. But he has biased the whole thing toward abstractions, and his whole psychology has turned into intellectualism. We must develop an ability to see, on the one side, the unity of thinking, feeling and willing and, on the other side, the differences between them.

If, having sufficiently prepared ourselves, we now consider everything connected with human willing and desiring, then we can compare this willing with something that stands farther away in the life of the soul, namely, the intellect. We can ask ourselves, "How is the life of willing, the life of desiring, related to the intellectual life of concepts?" Slowly we realize that a developmental difference exists between willing and thinking, a developmental difference like the one that exists, for example, between the child and the elderly person. The elderly person develops from the child; thinking develops from willing. The two are not so different from one another that we can put them next to each other and say, the one is this, the other is that. Rather, they are different from one another in the way that developmental stages are different. We will first be able to correctly understand the life of the human soul in its unity when we know if an apparently pure desire, a pure willing that appears in the human soul, is a youthful expression of the life of the soul. There the soul is living in a youthful stage. If intellectual activity appears, if ideas appear, then the soul is living in the condition that presupposes an unfolding of the will, a development of the will. The life of feeling exists in between, just as the thirty-five-year-old person exists between the child and the elderly person. Through feeling, the will develops itself into intellectual life. Only when we grasp that willing, feeling and thinking, in their liveliness, in their divergence, are not three separate capacities of the soul, which Herbart resisted but which has never been properly corrected, do we come to a true grasp of human soul life.

However, our observations indeed easily deceive us if we view the life of the soul from this standpoint. Our observations easily deceive us because in this life between birth and death we can never allow our understanding to remain fixed if we use a living awareness of life as a basis. Those who want to believe that life between birth and death proceeds so that intelligence simply develops out of the will, stand on quite shaky ground. We see how intelligence gradually reveals itself out of basic human nature in the growing child. We can only develop intelligence, including the intelligence developed through education, if we are conscious that what children experience after birth is the idea, the consequence, of their experiences before birth, before conception. We only understand what develops into will during life between birth and death if we are aware that people go through the Portals of Death into a spiritual life, and there further develop the will.

We cannot really educate people if we do not take their total life into account. We cannot really educate people if we merely say to ourselves, "We want to develop what the future will need." In saying this, we do not take the constitution of human nature into account. Every child, from day to day, from week to week, from year to year, reveals through its physical body what had developed in the life before birth, before conception. We will never gain a correct view of the will if we do not become conscious that what begins to appear as will is only a seed which develops in the physical body as in a fertile soil, but does not come to full fruition until we lay aside the physical body. Certainly, we must develop moral ideas in people. However, we must be clear that these moral ideas, embedded in the will as they are between birth and death, do not mean nearly as much as they seem, for their real life first begins when we leave this body.

Modern people are still shocked that, to obtain a complete understanding of humanity, it is necessary to consider all that humans endure before birth and after death along with what presently lives in people. This is necessary if we are to achieve an integration of humans into the whole, including into the temporal world. If we do not include that, if we consider people the way modern anthropology considers them—only in their existence between birth and death—then we do not consider the complete person, but only a portion. We cannot educate this portion of a person for the simple reason that we stand before the growing child and try to educate something we don't understand. Characteristics want to develop according to the standards set by the experiences before birth, but no one pays attention to that. We cannot solve the riddle of the child because we have no idea about what is in the child from the life before birth, and we do not know the laws of development that first unfold when the child has gone through death.

A main requirement of modern education must be to work out of a science that takes the whole person into account, not one that claims to see the pupil instead of the subject matter, but sees only a faceless abstraction of the person. What we will use as the basis of the educational system is truly not one-sided mysticism, but simply a full observation of all of human nature and the will to really comprehend the whole person in education. If we tend, as Herbart does, toward the one-sided development of the intellect, then the formation of willing and feeling must remain untrained and undeveloped. In this case, we would believe that through the acquisition, creation and development of certain ideas, we can call forth the restraint and support of the ideas he speaks of when he speaks of feeling and willing. We cannot do that; we can only develop the outdated will, that is, through an intellectual education we can only develop intellectualism. We can develop feeling only through a relationship that itself arises out of a genuine rapport between teacher and pupil. We can develop the will only by becoming conscious of the mysterious threads that unconsciously connect the pupil and teacher. Creating abstract principles of education for the development of feeling and willing can lead to nothing if we disregard the necessity of permeating the teachers and instructors with characteristics of mind and will that can work spiritually—not through admonition, that is physical—on the pupil. So, too, we must not build the educational relationship one-sidedly on intellectualism. It must depend wholly upon the person-to-person relationship. Here you see that it is necessary to expand everything that is connected with education. We must, therefore, take into account that the intimate relationship between teacher and pupil *can* be formed, thus raising the statement, "We should not simply pass on information, we should educate the pupil," above the empty phrase. We can do this only if we become conscious that, if this is the goal, the teacher's life cannot depend upon political or economic whims. It must stand on its own two feet to work out of its own impulses, its own conditions.

The leaders of modern society only vaguely feel what Anthroposophy and the realm of the Threefold Social Organism assert. Since these leaders of modern society uncourageously shun the thought of allowing themselves really to grasp life, to grasp it in the way striven for through anthroposophically oriented spiritual science, they are also unable to recognize, even with all good will, the full nature of human beings. They cannot bring themselves to say, "We must base the educational system in particular upon a real recognition and a real experiencing of spiritual impulses." It is interesting to see the leaders agonizing their way through modern culture toward a freeing of the educational system. It is interesting to see how they are unable to free themselves, because they really do not know what to do; they live in contradiction because they want reform through a science founded upon outdated concepts.

I have a book in front of me, entitled *Entwicklungs-Psychologie und Erziehungswissenschaft* [Developmental psychology and pedagogy], by Dr. Johann Kretzschmar, who actually wants to do something new in instruction, who feels that instructional methods do not really fit the social mood of the times. Let's examine something characteristic about this man. He says:

> If we proceed in this way from the standpoint of independent, investigative science [and here he means a pedagogy that is thoroughly based upon an outdated science] then not only will the teacher training and school work be influenced, but also the position of the teacher, the pedagogue, in the state, in the school administration. First of

all, it is obvious, in principle, that the teacher, like a doctor, must hold a position of trust regarding the state and community. They must admit that education—just like health care—is something in which primarily the opinion of the scientifically trained expert must be the standard, not the wishes of political and religious parties; further, the leadership of the school is less an administrative activity than a scientific function...

What does this man feel, then? He feels that administrative activity, however much it may be a state function, cannot extend so far into education that there is only an administrative knowledge, with too little understanding of human nature, in the impulses of the instructors and teachers. He would like to see administration replaced with what we can learn scientifically about human nature. Therefore, from a vague feeling he says:

...further, the leadership of the school is less an administrative activity than a scientific function, that consequently cannot be prescribed in every detail by means of official decrees. Communities and the state must have full trust that the faculty will competently carry out their responsibilities, that they are aware of the full extent of their duties and are, thus, completely independent of external influences. This trust is revealed in that—insofar as the internal affairs of the school organization are concerned—along with the directors, the teachers will also come into their own, that is, the teachers will not be considered as subordinates, as employees. The proper appreciation of pedagogical activity will thus show itself in the question of the regulation of school supervision. Neither the theologian nor the academic can be considered as the suitable person for the leadership and supervision of the school; [One only wonders then, how does he not get around to understanding that he, too, cannot be appointed as a school supervisor by the state, that he, too, must be removed from his position in the school system?] both must be completely placed in the hands of experts, of pedagogues. [Yes, why shouldn't those from the pedagogical field direct the schools first hand? Why is there first the detour through something that, in principle, cannot relevantly partake in the discussions!] That the institutions for handicapped persons, the schools for the mentally retarded, etc., should be directed neither by ministers nor by doctors, hardly needs any particular proof. Most important now is the influence of the faculty on educational legislation...

The influence of the faculty on educational legislation will quite certainly be the greatest when the teachers themselves make the laws concerning education in the self-administered cultural realm of the Threefold Social Organism.

You see in all this a dull movement toward what only the impulse of the Threefold Social Organism has the courage to really want to implant in the outside world. The best of modern people recognize the need for what the impulse of the Threefold Social Organism wants. But, the stale air of today's public life constricts the spiritual breathing of these modern people. They never complete their thoughts because prejudices weld everything together in the unified state. And so, one can read that the legislation

> ... will have to point out that the influence of the school on the home must be supported and strengthened by the state, that under certain circumstances, difficult or anti-education parents are to be forced into the proper rearing of their children. The school board would thus look to the

state to sanction not only the board's overseeing of the school system, but also the support and protection of the teachers...

People wonder, "Yes, why shouldn't the teachers be able to do all this?" As I just said, they do not sense the free breath that permits free cultural life. The enfeeblement of thought in the old unified state has brought people so far that they don't even think about what an absurdity it is to want the state to first order, then protect and support what the cultural members of the social organism should manage. Isn't the idea that the teacher "should be protected and supported by the state" so typical? That is the same as saying, "We don't dare to bring about this condition which would be so desirable; we want to be forced." But the motivation does not come. For on that side from which we should expect it, exists no understanding—obviously, quite justifiably—for what really should happen.

This increased influence of the state upon child rearing [now he wants an even greater influence by the state upon what the teacher and educator should do] lies quite logically in the direction of historical development.

Yes, it really does lie in the direction of historical development, but for it to be healthy, historical development must take a course different from the one that it is now on. Consider, for instance, a plant that, in the sense of Goethean metamorphosis, would only produce green leaves, never going on from the green foliage leaf to the colored flower leaf. Such a plant would never reach the goal of its development. In a similar sense, we must take account of the fact that historical development cannot always continue in the same way, but rather that one stage of development must supersede another.

There was a time when the state had no direct interest in the education system, a time when it first expressed an interest in compulsory schooling and formal education. The modern state, regarded as a constitutional state in that the people are directly involved in legislation, must put particular value not only upon the political, but also upon the general education of its members.

Inasmuch as the educational possibilities of the school are limited, the state must expand its influence into all areas of upbringing, to the family and environment of the child. [Now the state should be a co-educator in parallel to what cultural life is itself able to do. You see how you can have vague feelings that are correct, and how you can arrive at a point of view that is in such contrast to that toward which you, from a healthy point of view, should strive.] That area of pedagogy that is of the greatest value to the state is, of course, pedagogical sociology; [Now he wants to make social life the yardstick of pedagogy, while, in actuality, the social desires of people must arise from correct education so that they are available for the rehabilitation of social life.] it shows, on the one hand, the influence of education on public welfare and, on the other hand, sheds light on the extent to which the development of the child is not simply a matter of systematic education, but also depends upon the co-educators. The school board must also be reminded time and again of the importance of pedagogical sociology, since the Board's advice will be all the more indispensable to the state as the state's influence upon education increases.

Here Kretzschmar understands that the state will find it increasingly more necessary to pay attention to education. Yet, we shall not hear directly from an institution that can be developed out of the school system itself; rather, the state should do it. Then he points out that the state can also give orders. Thus, what in our time actually demands to develop freely and independently is to be curtailed.

There is something particularly interesting in this book. Obviously a person as well-intentioned as Kretzschmar is will also be aware that we must change teacher training. He notes that in the schools of education, not everything is as he would like to have it. He notices it, and says that there is much that we must change. He notes that the universities treat pedagogy as a secondary subject, but pedagogy includes much that, in his opinion, should not be treated in a subsidiary fashion. Rather, we must integrate it into the universities as an independent department. Now, he thinks, the four schools have already been augmented. The School of Natural Science has been formed out of the School of Philosophy, the School of Political Science has been formed out of the School of Law. He wonders if it would be possible to expand one of these schools to include Pedagogy.

There are universities today that, along with the four main schools—that is, the Theological, Philosophical, Medical and Law Schools—also have Political Science and Natural Science Schools. Kretzschmar thinks that the creation of an independent School of Education could lead to all kinds of problems. With which school could Pedagogy be joined? It is so characteristic that he concludes that it is most appropriate to join Pedagogy with Political Science and create a new School of Political-Educational Science!

You see, so great is the pressure working on people that everything should emanate from the state, that such an enlightened man as this believes it best to make pedagogy a part of political science. I have said it here before: people continually strive to be not what they are by nature, but what they can be through the blessing of the state. They are not to be free citizens, but people somehow included with their rights in the state. People strive to be members of the state. That fulfills the thought, "People must be educated so that they may become good members of the state." Where should we better place pedagogy than as a part of political science? It is interesting that a man who has such completely correct feelings concerning what should happen draws such opposite conclusions from his premises than you would think.

Today I have characterized the resistance against which we will have to struggle if we are to create a school such as the Waldorf School is to be. It goes against the thoughts of people, even the best people. It must oppose them, for otherwise it would not work in the direction of future development. We must work in the direction of future development, particularly in the areas of culture and education.

We have no desire to create a school with a one-sided philosophical viewpoint. Anyone who believes that we wish to form an "Anthroposophical school" or spreads that idea, believes or spreads a malignment. That is not at all what we want, and we will prove it. If people try to meet us as we try to meet everything, then religious instruction in the Waldorf School for Protestant children will be taught by the local Protestant minister, Catholic instruction given by the Catholic priest, Jewish by the rabbi. That is, we will not engage in propagating any particular point of view. We do not want to bring the content of Anthroposophy into our school; we want something else. Anthroposophy is life, it is not merely a theory. Anthroposophy can go into the formation, into the practice of teaching. Insofar as Anthroposophy can become pedagogical, to the extent that, through Anthroposophy, teachers can learn skills to teach arithmetic better than it has been taught, to teach writing, languages, geography better than they have been taught, to the extent that a method should be created for this school through

Anthroposophy—to this extent we strive to bring in Anthroposophy. We aspire to methodology, to instructional reform. That is what will result from a true knowledge of the spiritual. We will teach reading, we will teach writing, and so forth, in a manner appropriate to human nature.

Thus, we can turn our backs on what people will probably insinuate, that through a school we want to subject children to anthroposophical propaganda. We do not want that. For we know quite well that already the resistance we need to overcome is nearly immeasurable. We will only strive to teach as well as it is possible to teach when enlivened by anthroposophical impulses. Thus it will not disturb us if we must meet certain demands that come from here and there, for example, that people designated by the confessions must give religious instruction for the different confessions.

2

The Spirit of the Waldorf School

STUTTGART—AUGUST 31, 1919

LAST WEEK, I attempted to explain various aspects of the basis of the Waldorf School. I have already pointed out that this school did not appear out of the blue, that we must consider it in the context of modern education. However, we may put into the current stream of education only what conforms with our goals and our perceptions. I have suggested the difficulties that await a true art of education in our time. Today I will point out—of course, I can do this only in a general way—some things that will enable you to see the spirit from which an art of education may now develop. Quite possibly, due to people's diverse backgrounds, a vague feeling, or even an almost conscious idea, already exists that our educational system is in need of change. The truly correct reformation of the social future of humanity depends upon the creation of a genuine art of education equal to the cultural tasks of the present and near future.

The primary concern is to have a suitable faculty, particularly for the younger age groups. What the teachers bring to the children, the impulse out of which they practice their art, is a very essential quality. Contemplating this more closely, we find much in the present time that resists the proper understanding of this quality. Of course, it is natural that the teachers, the educators, first attend the institutions of learning that have developed out of the more or less scientific consciousness of the present. However, this modern scientific consciousness is such that it does not provide any means of truly understanding the developing human. We find just in this point the first task necessary for founding the Waldorf School. I said in my last lecture here that we have already gathered the faculty of the Waldorf School, and that this future faculty is pursuing a pedagogical-didactic preparation. Our primary task is first to enable the teachers to find the proper attitude for understanding developing human nature and how it appears in childhood. Secondly, we want to bring them to the point where they can practice the art of education out of this insight. In the present time it is necessary to carve out a quite new—new for society at large—understanding and knowledge of humanity.

We, with our scientific mentality, are proud of our methods of experimentation and observation. These methods have led to great triumphs in the fields of natural science. However, many of our contemporaries who are close to the educational system feel that these same experimental and observational methods are incapable of finding an approach to education. Many people with a certain level of perception have asked, "What can we do to rightly use the developmental capacities that arise in the successive stages of the child's life?" I need only point out a few things to show that some educators already have the desire to really understand the development of the child, but that due to the current scientific mentality they stand helplessly before such questions. Already in 1887, for example, the educator Sallwürk drew attention to the discovery of a certain natural law that holds true during the development of an organism. According to this Recapitulation Theory, as it was named by the recently deceased Ernst Haeckel, the embryonic development of each individual human follows the history of development of the animal kingdom. During the first weeks of embryonic development, the human is similar to the lower animals, and then rises until it develops into a human. The individual development is a shortened repetition of a long development in the world at large. Educators have now asked themselves, "Can something similar also hold true for the mental development of the individual child? Also, can education find any help in a rule patterned after the Recapitulation Theory?"

You see, an effort already exists, not simply to begin teaching, but to gain insight into the development of the growing human. It was, for instance, obvious to say that all of humanity has gone through the time of the prehistoric cultures; then followed cultures such as those handed down to us through the writings of the ancient oriental cultures; then came the Greek and Roman cultures, followed by the developments of the Middle Ages, and so forth, right up to the present time.

Can we say that each human as a child repeats the stages of human cultural development during childhood? Can we, by observing the course of history, obtain an insight into the development of the individual child? Sallwürk emphatically argued in his 1887 book *Gesinnungsunterricht und Kulturgeschichte* [The training of character and cultural history] that educators could not gain any help from such ideas. Even before that, the pedagogue Theodor Vogt, a follower of the Herbart school of thought, suggested that at present we are powerless to answer such pedagogical questions. In 1884 he said that if there were a science of comparative history in the sense of comparative linguistics, it could perhaps give us insight into child rearing comparable to the insight into the historical development of animals found in the Recapitulation Theory. However, he admitted that such a historical science did not exist. The pedagogue Rein echoed his words in 1887, and so things still lie in superficial pedagogy and the superficial art of education today.

Regarding such efforts and the discussions about such efforts, you can rightly say, "Yes, concerning what is necessary for the development of the growing child, shouldn't we, as educators, begin from the standpoint of a healthy human intuition, instead of allowing abstract science to dictate to us?" You would be right in raising such an objection. This objection also arises, if we consider the matter a bit more thoroughly, because the abstractions of that science based upon the methods of the present understanding of nature can tell us nothing concerning the development of the human spirit and the human soul. We work in vain if we attempt to use this. No one can become a true artist in education simply out of undeveloped human intellect and intuition. We need something that gives us insight. Just here we see that a new understanding of humans is needed as the foundation for a real future art of education. Normal science does not provide even the basis for such an understanding of humans. It must be gained by recognizing the human spirit and by recognizing the development of the human spirit within human history. We must have a much broader point of view than that of modern mechanistically oriented natural science.

If we observe the growing child, we first find—I have often remarked on this—that a relatively long developmental period lies between birth and the change of teeth, around seven years of age. If we compare what works during this time in the soul of the child with what develops in the time between the change of teeth and sexual maturity, a major difference is apparent. The child's orientation until the change of teeth is to imitate what it sees, hears and perceives in its surroundings. In this period, the child is an imitator. From the age of seven until fifteen, from the change of teeth until sexual maturity, the child's orientation is affected by the authority in its surroundings. For the most part, the child does not simply imitate, but wants to hear from adults what is right, what is good. He or she wants to believe in the judgment of adults; instinctively, the child wants authority. The child can develop only if he or she can develop this belief.

If we look further, however, we can see that shifts emerge during these major stages of life. We see, for example, that a clear shift occurs around three years of age, in the period between birth and the change of teeth, when children develop, for the first time, a clear feeling of their own selves. In later life, that event marks the earliest point they can remember; earlier experiences recede into the sleep of childhood. Much else appears around the same time in the development of the child, so we can say that, although the child is essentially an imitator in the first seven years of life, there is a turning point around the middle of this period that must be considered in early child rearing.

Two important phases lie in the period between the change of teeth and sexual maturity, that is, during that time in the child's life when elementary education takes place. When the child approaches approximately nine years of age, those who are able will observe a great change in the child's development. In the first seven years of life, the child is an imitator. Children tend toward a feeling for authority after the change of teeth, but some earlier desires to imitate remain. Thus, until the age of nine, the need to imitate their surroundings continues, but now it is mixed with the need to allow authority to take effect. If we observe which capacities in the child's life arise out of the depths of human nature, then we find (as I said, I can merely touch upon these things today) through further consideration and observation, that the capacities that appear in this period between seven and nine years of age must be used to teach the child what naturally occurs as the beginnings of reading and writing. We should use these beginnings in the instruction of reading and writing so that only what is in harmony with the need to imitate and the need for authority is called upon. If we are artists in educating and can work, on the one hand, with the subject material and, on the other hand, with the emerging need for authority and the receding need to imitate, so that all of it harmonizes, then we create something in the child that has lasting power throughout life until death. We develop something that cannot be made up later, because each stage of life develops its own capacities. Certainly, you can say that many teachers have instinctively oriented themselves according to such laws. That is true, but it will not suffice in the future, for in the future, such things must be raised to consciousness.

Around the age of nine, everything that enables the child to go beyond people into an understanding of nature begins to develop. Before this time, the child is not very well suited to understand nature as such. We could say that until the age of nine, the child is well suited to observe the world in a moralizing manner. The teacher must meet this moralizing need of the child without becoming pedantic. Certainly, many teachers already act instinctively in this area.

If you examine the didactic instructions of the present, which should tend to relate the subject matter to human nature, then you could be driven to despair. A certain correct instinct is there, but these instructions are so narrow-minded and banal that they dreadfully harm the developing child. We would do well at this stage if we consider, for instance, animals or plants in a way such that a certain moralizing appears. For example, you can bring fables to children in a way that helps them to understand the animal world. You should be careful not to bring such "pablum" during the main lesson, as is so often done. Above all, you should take care not to tell a story to the children and then to follow it with all kinds of explanations. You destroy everything you want to achieve through telling the story by following it with interpretations. Children want to take stories in through feeling. Without outwardly showing it, they are dreadfully affected in their innermost being if they must listen afterwards to the often quite boring explanations.

What should we do in this situation, if we do not want to go into the real details of the art of storytelling? We might say, "Leave out the explanation and simply tell the children the story." Fine. Then the children will not understand the story and will surely not enjoy it if they do not understand it. If we want to speak Chinese to people, we must first teach them Chinese; otherwise they cannot have the right relationship to what we tell them in Chinese. Thus, we gain nothing by saying, "Leave out the explanations."

You must try to provide an explanation *first*. When you want to tell the children a story such as "The Wolf and the Lamb," simply speak with the children about the wolf's and the lamb's characteristics. (We could also apply this to plant life.) As much as possible, speak of these characteristics in relationship to people. Gather everything that you feel will help the children form pictures and feelings that will then resonate when you read the story. If, in an exciting preliminary talk, you offer what you would give afterward as an explanation, then you do not kill the sensations as you would in giving that explanation afterward. On the contrary, you enliven them. If the children have first heard what the teacher has to say about the wolf and the lamb, then their sensations will be all the more lively, and they will have all the more delight in the story. Everything that is necessary for understanding should happen beforehand. The children should not hear the story first. When they hear the story, you must bring them to the heights of their souls for them to understand it. This process must conclude in reading the story, telling the tale, doing nothing more than allowing the children's sensations, already evoked, to take their course. You must allow the children to take their feelings home.

Until the age of nine, it is necessary to form the instruction in this way, to relate everything to people. If we have the sensitivity to observe the transition that occurs around nine years of age, we will know that then the child is first capable of going out into the world of nature. However, the child still relates nature to people. If we describe nature without any relationship to people, it is not yet comprehensible to the nine-year-old child. We only deceive ourselves if we believe that the children understand the conventional descriptions offered as instruction in natural science. We must, of course, take up the study of nature when the child reaches nine years of age, but we must always relate it to people. Particularly in the study of nature, we should not begin with the idea of nature as something external to humans, but always begin with humanity itself; we should always put people in the center.

Let us assume that we want a child older than nine to understand the difference between lower animals, higher animals and people—then we begin with people. We compare the lower animals with the human; we compare the higher animals with the human. If we have described the human in terms of form, in terms of daily tasks, then we can apply what we know about humans to the lower and higher animals. The child understands that.

We should not worry too much that we are speaking above the child's level of understanding. (Today we sometimes speak above the level of adult understanding.) We do not speak above the child's level of understanding if, for example, we say—of course, with enthusiasm and with a real understanding of the subject—"Look at the lower animals!" Let's say that we give the child the chance to see a squid. Then, always using the appropriate terms, we go on to show with which parts of the ideal human the squid is most closely related. The child can quickly understand that the squid is most closely related to the human head. It is in reality so; the lower animals have only simple forms, but the human head repeats the forms that find their simplest expression in the lower animals. The human head is only endowed in a more complicated way than the lower animals. What we find in the higher animals, for example, mammals, can only be compared with what we find in the human torso. We should not compare the higher animals with the human head, but with the torso. If we go on to the human limbs, then we must say, "Look at the human limbs; in their form they are uniquely human. The way the arms and hands are formed—as appendages to the body in which the soul-spirit in us can move freely—such a pair of limbs is not found anywhere in the entire animal kingdom!" If we speak of the monkey's four hands, this is really an improper manner of speaking since their nature is to serve in holding, in moving the body along. In the human we see a remarkable differentiation of the hands and feet, the arms and legs. What makes a human really a human? Certainly not the head; it is only a more perfect form of what we find already in the lower animals. What we find in the lower animals is further developed in the human head. What makes a human, human, what puts the human far above the animal world, are the limbs.

Of course, you cannot bring what I have just shown you to children in the same form. You translate it so that the child by and by learns to feel such things out of experience. Then, through your teaching you can clear away endless amounts of what, for quite mysterious reasons, currently spoils our moral culture. Our present moral culture is so often spoiled because people are so proud and arrogant concerning the head. Whereas, people could be proud of their limbs—though they would not be if the limbs were better developed, and this can be proven—that serve to work, that serve to put them in the world of social order.

Natural scientific instruction concerning the animal world can, in an unconscious way, bring the correct feelings about the relationship of people to themselves and about social order into human nature. This shows that the pedagogical question has a much deeper meaning than we generally believe today, that it concerns the great, all-encompassing cultural questions. It also provides information about how to teach science to children after the age of nine. You can relate everything to humanity, but in such a way that nature appears everywhere alongside humans and humans appear as a great condensation of nature. Teachers can give the child much if they maintain this point of view until about the age of twelve.

Around twelve years of age, an important change begins in the development of the child. At the age of twelve, thirteen, fourteen—it is different in each child—that which sexual maturity expresses comes into play, namely, the ability to judge, judgment. Judgment comes into play and must work together with the reduction in the need for authority. The teacher must harmoniously handle the need for authority and judgmental powers during this age. We must treat the subject material in this way.

This is the time when we may begin to bring in those natural scientific and, in particular, physical facts that are completely independent of humans, for instance, the refraction of light and such. It is at this age that the understanding of how to use nature in relationship to humans begins. Until the twelfth year, the child, through inner necessity, wants to understand nature from the standpoint of a human, no longer moralizing, but in the way I just described to you. After the twelfth year, the child tends to observe what is independent of people, but to relate it back to people. You develop something that the child does not forget again when you, let us say, explain the refraction of light through a lens, and then continue on to its application to people, the refraction of light in the eye, the whole inner structure of the eye. You can teach this to a child of this age.

You see, the true curriculum results from an understanding of the stages of human life. The children themselves tell us, if we can really observe them, what they want to learn in a particular stage of life. However, we cannot derive these results from modern natural science. Using natural scientific facts, you simply do not come to the point of view that shows the immeasurable importance of that Rubicon in life that lies around the ninth year, or the other Rubicon in life that lies around the twelfth year. We must bring these things forth out of the entirety of human nature. This entirety of human nature includes body, soul and spirit; modern science, although it believes itself capable of saying something about soul and spirit, actually limits itself to the body. The way such things are often discussed today—whether to emphasize academics or morality in teaching, whether to teach people more according to their abilities, or to see that they learn more about science because it will be needed later for a job, or so that they can take their place in society—these questions appear childish when we get to know the deeper basis from which education must emanate. How the individual relates to all of human development is not understood by natural science. However a spiritual comprehension of human developmental history does understand it.

Let us consider the following law, which is just as much a law as the laws of natural science, but which the methods of modern science do not comprehend. If we go back—you will find these things fully developed in my writings—to the ancient times of humanity, we find that people remained capable of development into very old age, capable of development in the way that we are now capable only during our early childhood. If we go back to these ancient times, we find that people said to themselves, "When I am thirty-five years old," or in still earlier times, "When I am forty-two years old, I will with certainty go through changes connected with the development of my body that will make me into another person." Just as at the change of teeth we go through something connected with the development of the body which makes us into another person, just as at sexual maturity we go through something connected with the development of the body which makes us into another person, so in ancient times did people go through such things into very old age. In the course of time, human development has lost this. Today, in childhood we cannot look at an older person and say, to the same extent as was possible in ancient times, "I will be happy to be so old some day, because this person has experienced something that, due to my present stage of bodily development, is not yet possible for me." The progress of human development is such that we bring a bodily development to ever fewer older stages of life.

Those able to observe such things know that, for example, in Greek times still, people in their thirties clearly perceived, as we today in our youth perceive, things not connected with the physical body. Today such perceptions are at most possible for people before the age of twenty-seven. In the future, this age will be even younger. This is the direction of human development, that the natural, the basic, development of the individual continues only to an ever-younger age. That is a fundamental law. Our cultural development is directly connected with this fundamental law, in that reading and writing appear at a particular age, whereas, in ancient times, they were not there. This is connected with humanity's dependency upon ever-younger stages of natural development. Those who can then look further for such clues concerning human development, which we can gain only from an inclusive knowledge, will know how the longings of a Theodor Vogt, a Rein, a Sallwürk can be satisfied. The current mechanistic orientation of science does not have even the possibility of knowing something like this human life, in which natural development is condensed into ever younger stages of life. It does not have even the possibility of creating a truly comparative historical science that could give clues about how to recognize people's relationship to cultural development. However, those who look further know that people, as they are born, have, of course, characteristics appropriate to their epoch, that they are part of a comprehensive human development. If we develop the aptitudes people already have, then, simply because these people are a part of human development, what we should develop is, in a formal sense, developed. If we recognize reality, then much of what causes such a furor today—whether to do things this way or that—becomes only an abstract rambling. This attitude of confrontation resolves itself in a true, a real, attitude of compromise.

This, you see, is what we would like to develop in the Waldorf School faculty, to create in at least one place something for the future. We hope that the teachers will correctly recognize people and the relationship of people to modern culture, and that they will be inspired by this knowledge, by this feeling, to a will to work together with the child. Then true educational artists will emerge. Upbringing is never a science, it is an art. Teachers must be absorbed in it. They can only use what they know as a starting point for the art of education.

We should not ramble on too much about the needs of teachers to have quite specific capabilities. These capabilities are more widespread than we think—only at present they are not very well developed. We need only the perseverance to develop them in the teachers in the right way, through a strong spiritual science. Then, we will find that what we call teaching ability is more widespread than we think.

You see, this is connected with something else again. Today, in theory, we are often warned against too much abstraction in instruction; but we still instinctively make these abstractions. It will concern those who see through these things that the plans and ideas for reform presently so common will make instruction more abstract than it is now. It will become worse in spite of all the beautiful ideas contained in these reform plans. If we study the stages of human development correctly—first, the long stages up to the change of teeth and to sexual maturity, and then the shorter stages up to the development of a feeling of self and the sense of people separate from nature—if we study these epochs correctly, so that we do not tritely define them, but obtain an artistic, intuitive picture of them, then we can first understand how greatly the developing child is damaged when intellectual education is steered in the wrong direction. We should always emphasize the need to educate people as whole beings. But we can only bring up people as whole beings if we know their separate parts, including the soul and spirit, and understand how to put them together. We can never educate people as whole beings if in education we allow thinking, feeling and willing to interact chaotically. We can educate people as whole beings only if we intuitively know what the characteristics of thinking, of feeling, of willing are. Then, we can allow these powers of the human being to interact correctly in the soul and the spirit.

When people today discuss such things, they tend to fall into extremes. When people realize that intellect is too prominent, that our intellects are too strongly developed, they become enthusiastic about eradicating this imbalance, and say, "Everything depends upon the development of will and feeling." No, everything depends upon developing all three elements! We must develop people's intellect, feeling and will in the right way, so that they can understand how to let those three elements of life interact correctly. If we are to develop the intellectual element correctly, then during the elementary school period we must give children something that can grow with them, that can develop as a whole. Understand me correctly, particularly on this point, for it is an important point. Think about it. You develop in children until the age of fourteen those ideas that you have carefully defined so the children know how they are to think them. But, just through the good definitions you have given them, you have often given them ideas that are quite stiff, that cannot grow with the person. People must grow from the age of fourteen to twenty, from the age of twenty to twenty-five, and so forth, and at the same time, their ideas must grow along with them. The ideas must be able to grow in parallel. If your definitions are too well formed, people grow, but their ideas do not grow with them. You guide intellectual development in the wrong direction. Then in cultural life, people will be unable to do anything except remember the ideas that you so carefully gave them. That would be wrong. Children's ideas should grow in parallel with their own development. Their ideas should grow so that what they learned at the age of twelve is, at the age of thirty-five, as different from what it was when they first learned it, as people in their physical bodies at the age of thirty-five are different from what they were at the age of twelve. That is to say, in intellectual development, we must not bring something well-formed and dead, but teach something living, something that has life in it and can change. Thus, we will define as little as possible. If we want to bring ideas to a child, we will depict them from as many points of view as possible. We will not say, "What is a lion? A lion is such and such." Rather, we will depict a lion from many different points of view—we will instill living, moving ideas that will then live with the child. In this regard, modern education does much damage.

People must live through their earthly existence, and often the ideas that we instill in them die and remain as soul corpses; they cannot live. We cannot get to the root of these things with the crude concepts developed by modern pedagogy. A very different spiritual impulse must imbue this pedagogy. That is something we strive for in the Waldorf School. We try to give pedagogy a new basis from which to consider such things psychologically. We are completely convinced that an understanding of human beings cannot arise out of the old principles, and that, therefore, these cannot be the principles of a pedagogy based upon psychology. We cannot form this psychology of the developing human with the methods that are so common today.

You see, when we can really, correctly, observe such things, then we throw light on many secondary concepts that we hold to be very important today. We can easily understand them once we understand the main concepts. There is today, for instance, so much nonsense concerning the importance of play in the education of children. In considering the importance of play, we often forget the most important thing, namely that if play is strongly regulated and children are made to direct their play toward a particular goal, then it is no longer play. The essence of play is that it is free. If, however, you make play really play, as is necessary for instruction, then you will not fall prey to the foolish expression, "Instruction should be just a game." Then you will look more for the essential in the rhythm that comes into the life of the child when you allow play and work to alternate.

In training the mind and training feeling, we must give particular attention to the individual characteristics of the child. As teachers, we must be capable of forming the instruction so that the child does not simply receive something intellectual in the instruction, but enjoys the instruction in an aesthetic way. We cannot achieve this if the ideas appeal only to the intellect. We can do this if we, as teachers, relate to the children's feelings in such varied ways that we actually elicit the children's expectations of the subject, which we then fulfill. We can do this if we arouse hopes that, both large and small, we fulfill—if we develop every positive attribute of the children that can play a role in an aesthetic understanding of their surroundings. You can meet the child's aesthetic needs if you bring yourself into a correct relationship to the child's feelings, if you don't tritely "sell" nature studies, as is done nowadays: "Look, there is a mouse. The mouse runs. Was there ever a mouse at home? Have you ever seen a mousehole?" Of course, today instruction in nature study is not given in such extreme tastelessness, but similarly. People have no idea how much good taste, that is, the aesthetic experiencing of children, is damaged through what people nowadays call nature studies. We will develop taste only by steering the child's interest to large, inclusive views. For the proper unfolding of the mind, of feeling, taste must rule in instruction and in the schools. Thus, we can develop a certain instinct for the essentials in education.

The intellect is at first the highest mental aspect in each of us; but if we develop it one-sidedly, without a concurrent development of feeling and will, then we also develop a tendency toward materialistic thinking. Although the intellect is our highest mental aspect during physical earthly life, intellect is directed toward materialism. Specifically, we should not believe that when we develop the intellect, we also develop people spiritually. As paradoxical as that sounds, it is nevertheless true that we develop people's capacity to understand material things when we develop the intellect. By first tastefully, in an aesthetic way, developing the sensitivity, the feelings, we can direct the human intellect toward the soul aspects. We can give children a foundation for directing the intellect toward the spirit only insofar as we practice a development of will, even if we develop it only as physical dexterity. That so few people today tend to direct the intellect toward the spirit can only be a consequence of the fact that the will was so incorrectly trained during childhood.

How do we as teachers learn to develop will in the proper way? I recently pointed out that we learn to do it by allowing children to be artistically active. As early as possible, we should not only allow children to hear music, to see drawings and paintings, but also allow them to participate. Besides mere instruction in reading and writing—yes, we must develop instruction in reading and writing from artistic activities, writing from drawing, and so forth—besides all this, basic artistic activities must take place early in the education wherever possible. Otherwise, we will have weak-willed people. Directing youths toward what their later work will be comes in addition to this.

You see just how necessary it is in modern times that we come to a new understanding of humanity. This understanding can be the basis for a new way of educating, as much as this is possible within all the constraints that exist today. Because modern science does not comprehend these things, we must create something that leads in this direction through the Waldorf School.

It is urgently necessary that we do not allow ourselves to be deceived by much of what is said today. A week ago, I tried to explain the significance of the empty phrase for modern spiritual life. Empty phrases come into play particularly in educational reform plans. People feel good—and they believe that they are "very pedagogical"—when they repeatedly admonish others to raise people, not robots. But those who say this must first know what a real human is; otherwise this sentence becomes just an empty phrase. This is particularly so when the often-asked question, "To what end should we educate children?" is answered by, "To be happy and useful people." Those who say this mean people who are useful in the way the speakers find useful and happy in the way the speakers mean happy.

It is especially important that we form a foundation that allows us to understand what human beings really are. However, this cannot be done with the old prejudices of our world view. It can only come from a new understanding of the world. A new form of education will not develop if we do not have the courage to come to a new scientific orientation. What we see most often today are people who want everything conceivable, but not what is necessary to arrive at a new orientation in understanding the world. We have been searching for this new orientation for years by means of spiritual science. If many people have distanced themselves from it, that is because they find it too uncomfortable, or because they do not have the courage. But what we need for a real art of education can emerge only from a properly founded spiritual world view.

Think about the importance of what the teacher represents to the growing child. Basically, we people here on earth, if we are not to become petrified in one of the stages in our life, must continually learn from life. But, first we must learn to learn from life. Children must learn to learn from life in school so that, in later life, their dead ideas do not keep them from learning from life; so that, as adults, they are not petrified. What keeps eating at people today is that school gave them too little. Those who see through our deplorable social conditions know that they are largely connected with what I have just described. People do not have that inner hold on life that can come only when the right material is taught at the right time in school. Life remains closed if school does not give us the strength to open it. This is only possible if, in the early school years the teacher is the representation of life itself. The peculiarity of youth is that the gulf still exists between people and life. We must bridge this gulf. The young senses, the young intellect, the young mind, the young will are not yet so formed that life can touch them in the right way. Children meet life through the teacher. The teacher stands before the child as, later, life stands there. Life must be concentrated in the teacher. Thus, an intensive interest in life must imbue the teachers. Teachers must carry the life of the age in themselves. They must be conscious of this. Out of this consciousness can radiate what lively instruction and conduct must communicate to the pupils. To begin such a thing, teachers must no longer be miserably confined to the realm of the school; they must feel themselves supported by the whole breadth of modern society and how this interacts with the future, a future in which precisely teachers have the greatest interest. Under the present conditions and despite the present obstacles, we should try to do this in the school, as well as it can be done by people who bring the necessary prerequisites from their present lives. We should not work out of any one-sided interest, out of a preference for this or that, but rather work out of what speaks loudly and clearly to us as necessary for the development of present and future humanity. What in human developmental progress we see as necessary for our time should enter and strengthen instruction through the founding of the Waldorf School.

3

A Lecture for Prospective Parents
of the Waldorf School

STUTTGART—AUGUST 31, 1919

WHEN Mr. Molt first set out to found a school for the children of his employees, clearly his intention was to serve humanity in these difficult times. He chose a means which we must employ above all others when working to heal our social conditions. It is written in all your souls that we must create something new out of the conditions that we experience—the conditions that have developed over the past three or four centuries in the so-called civilized world. It must also have been deeply written in your souls that what we need above all to achieve other conditions is a different way of preparing human beings for a place in the world, through upbringing and education. What we need is a way untainted by the traditions of the past three or four centuries that are now reaching their zenith.

For the future, we expect a social structure much different from the one of the present. We have a right to expect that. We look lovingly at our children, at the next generation, and we, particularly those who are parents, often have misgivings in our hearts. How will our loved ones fit into a society that must be so different from that of the present? Will they be equal to the new social challenge coming to humanity? Will they be capable of contributing to the formation of society, so that those who come after us will have it other than we have had, will have, in a much different sense, a more humane existence than we have had?

Everyone feels that the question of upbringing and education is, in a profound sense, a question of the highest order.
This is particularly true in times like ours, times of sudden
change and transformation of society. We look back at the terrible times humanity has recently lived through in Europe, we
look upon the rivers of blood that have flowed, and we see the
great army of unhappy people, their bodies broken and their
souls shattered, which necessarily resulted from the unnatural
conditions of recent times. When we look upon all this, the
desire wells up in us to ask, "In the broadest sense, how must
we bring up people so that this will be impossible in the
future?" Out of this privation and misery, an understanding
must awaken for the role of education in restructuring human
social relations.

In principle, we hear this expressed from many sides. Yet,
we must ask ourselves, when people say this here and there, if
they always mean it in the correct sense. Today, people say
pleasant words about many things. These pleasant words do
not always arise from inner strength, nor above all else, from
inner truths that can put into practice the content of these
words. Today those people who are called upon to school and
educate our children come forth, offer their opinions and
notions, and say, "We know how children should be brought
up and educated. We should simply do it just as we have
always wanted, but have not been allowed to do—then the
right thing will occur." Behind those who so speak, we hear
those who feel themselves called to teach the teachers. They
assure us, "We have the right views about what teachers
should become. Just follow us. We will send the right teachers
into the world, so everything goes well in education." Yet,
when we look deeply into what has become of our social conditions, we want to shout to both these teachers and these
teachers of teachers, "You may mean well, but you do not

really know what you are talking about!" For nothing can help modern education, nothing can raise modern education to a better state, unless the teachers admit, "We come from the traditions formed during the past three or four centuries. We were trained in the way that leads humanity into such misfortune." In their turn, those who trained the teachers must admit, "We have not understood anything except how to give teachers the results of industrialism, statism, capitalism. Of course, we have delivered the present teachers, who fit into this present social configuration, this configuration that simply must change."

This means that, just as we demand a change, a transformation of the full spectrum of the present social structure for the future, we must also demand another art of education, and a different basis for this art!

In many respects, the question of education today is a question of teachers. Today, when we speak with those who want to become teachers and educators, we frequently sense the deep antisocial feeling lying within humanity. We speak with them about what education should become in the future. They say, "Yes, I have been saying that all along. We should raise children to be competent modern-day people. We should educate them to be useful people. We should not pay so much attention to vocational training, but more to the training of the whole person." They talk about such things and go away with the impression that they think just the same as we think. They think just the opposite!

Today, our antisocial life has come so far that people express opposites with the same words. This is what makes it so difficult to understand one another. Someone who truly thinks socially, thinks very differently from modern people satisfied with the old traditions. In the same way, we must think fundamentally differently about teaching and education when we attempt to solve the educational social question in a particular instance. We must think differently from those who believe we can base this change on their traditional educational methods. Truly, today we must think and perceive more thoroughly than many believe. In addition, we must be clear that we cannot create something new out of the old educational and scientific methods; education and science must themselves change.

This is adequate justification for us to begin this work of starting the Waldorf School with a course for the faculty. We have attempted to select for the faculty people who, at the least, are rooted in the old educational system to a greater or lesser degree—for one it is more, for another less. But, we were also intent on finding people who have the heart and soul for the reconstruction of our society and culture. We sought people who have the heart and soul for what it means to raise the children of today to be the people of tomorrow.

Our new teachers also must carry another conviction in their souls, namely, that from the time children enter school we may teach them only what the essence of humanity dictates. In this sense we want to found a unified school in the truest sense of the word. All we want to know in the growing child is the developing human being. We want to learn from the nature of the developing child how children want to develop themselves as human beings, that is, how their nature, their essence should develop to become truly human.

"That is just what we also want," the old teachers and educators of teachers tell us. "We have always tried to teach people, to consider, for example, the distinct personalities of the children."

Yes, we must reply, you have striven to train children to be what you perceived human beings to be, the kind of people you thought were necessary for the old political and economic life. We cannot do anything with this idea of "human beings";

and the future of humanity will not know what to do with it nor want to know. We need a fundamental renewal.

The first thing needed for the educational system of the future is a new understanding of humanity. The understanding of humanity that has swollen up out of the morass of materialism in the last centuries and has been dressed up in our higher schools of learning as the basis of human nature cannot be the basis of the art of education in the future. What we require is a new perception of human nature. We can derive this only from a new science. The science taught today, and also represented by those who teach, is only the reflection of older times. Just as a new epoch should come, so too should come a new science, a new way to train teachers, a new pedagogy built upon a new understanding of human beings. For just that reason, we pay particular attention to a real understanding of humanity in the course to prepare the faculty for the Waldorf School. We cherish the hope that the future teachers in the Waldorf School will come to know the developing human. We hope that they will give this embryonic human the capacities that the future will require of people who work in the socially formed human society. We sense that much of what the old way of teaching has said about humanity is just words. Today we study the true essence of human thought, so we can train the child in the right kind of thinking. We study the true basis of real human feeling, so that in the genuinely social community people bring forth justice based upon true human feeling. We study the essence of human will, so that this human will can embrace and permeate the newly formed economic life of the future. We do not study people in a materialistic, one-sided way; we study the body, soul and spirit of the human being, so that our teachers can train the body, soul and spirit of human beings. We do not speak of body, soul and spirit merely as words. We attempt to discover how the various stages of the human being result from one another. We look carefully at how the children are when they enter the school, and the faculty takes over from the parents.

How superficially the so-called educational sciences have observed this period of human growth! There is an important turning point in the life of a child; it lies around the age of seven, just about that year in which the child enters elementary school. It is just at that year when the teacher should take over the child from the parents for a portion of the further education. The external expression of this important period of life is the change of teeth; however, the new teeth are only an outward sign of the important change occurring within.

Certainly, you have already heard much about what we need to understand to properly comprehend social reforms, and so forth. However, many of you were probably still of the opinion, received from a study by the leading experts, that everything has already been taken care of for humanity in an admirable way. The most important things have not been done! Modern people find it quite strange, when we say that at the age when the child enters school, an inner revolution occurs in the human soul, in the whole being, which is only outwardly expressed only in the cutting of teeth. Until that time children are imitating beings, beings that bring through birth the urge to do everything as it is done around them. In these first years it is simply a part of human nature to allow ourselves to be trained by what we see in our surroundings. Just at the time of the cutting of teeth, something quite different begins to appear in human nature. The urge arises to learn from authority, to learn from those who already can do something. This urge lasts until the time of sexual maturity, until about fourteen or fifteen years of age. Thus, this natural drive fills the time in elementary school. We can properly teach in elementary school only if we have a thorough pedagogical understanding of this revolution within the child of seven. Here I have given you only a single example of what, compared to the old way, the new pedagogy must thoroughly observe and understand.

On the other hand, we need to know that around the age of nine new inner physical and spiritual strengths begin to come forth. If we were to teach prematurely what the curriculum foresees for the age after nine, the instruction, instead of helping, would damage the child for life.

We need a comprehensive understanding of human life if we want to practice a comprehensive, a true, pedagogy serving humanity. We must know how to teach before and after the children reach the age of nine. We may not, as old, gray-haired administrators from the school board do, set up the curriculum to take into account just any external consideration: this for the first grade; this for the second grade; this for the third grade; and so forth. Nothing that could really prepare the child for life will result. Human nature itself must teach us what we need to accomplish through education in each year of the child's life.

Consider for a moment that, as adults, you are still learning from life. Life is our great teacher. However, the ability to learn from life comes at the earliest at fifteen, sixteen or seventeen years of age. Then, we first stand face to face with the world in a way such that we can learn directly from the world. Until then, the teacher who faces us in the classroom is the world. It is the teacher we want to understand; it is the teacher we want to love; it is from the teacher we want to learn. The teacher should bring to us what is out there in the world. From the age of seven to fifteen years, there is an abyss between ourselves and the world. The teacher should bridge that gulf for us.

Can teachers who are not gripped by all that life has to give, who, embittered and soured by all that has been funneled into them, "teach grammar so, natural history so, and other subjects so," who do not concern themselves with what so agitates humanity in our time—can such teachers rightly depict and reveal to children all that life brings over the seven or eight years of elementary school? A new study of humanity, a new understanding of humanity is necessary. The faculty must develop a new enthusiasm out of this new understanding of humanity.

This shows you some of what we keep in mind in preparing for the children in our teaching seminars: to thoroughly understand humanity so that we can teach from human nature itself and send the child into life.

The second thing that we must develop as we work toward a more humane form of society is a social attitude of the teachers toward the children already in the school. This is a new love of humanity—an awareness of the interplay of forces between the teacher and pupil. Those forces cannot exist if the teacher does not enter into the art of teaching in a lively way.

Everyone agrees that the painter must learn to paint, that the musician must have command over a musical instrument and much more, that the architect must learn architecture. We set certain requirements so these people may become artists. We also must set these kinds of requirements for teachers who would become true human artists. We must set them seriously. To do so, we must understand that no present-day pedagogy and no present-day educational method gives the teacher what must first be found through a thorough study of humanity. We must find it so that a new love of humanity may come into the relationship between teacher and pupil. Our goal must be that teachers become true artists in their field.

Many things play a role. One teacher enters the classroom, and the children feel an aversion that lasts throughout the year; they would much rather be outside because what that teacher does with them is so unpleasant. Another teacher need only enter the classroom and, simply by being present, creates a bridge to each pupil. What makes such a difference? The teacher who makes such an adverse impression on the children goes into the school only to, as the saying goes, earn a living— in order to live. That teacher has acquired the superficial ability to drill the children, but goes just as unwillingly to school as the children and is just as happy when school ends. That teacher does the job mechanically.

I am not surprised that the majority of today's teachers view their work mechanically. Their understanding of humanity comes from the dead science that has arisen out of the industrial, statist and capitalist life of the past three or four centuries. That science has resulted in a dead art of education, at best a wistful form of education. We are striving for the understanding of humanity that we need to create the art of teaching in the Waldorf School. This vision of humanity, this understanding of humanity, so penetrates the human being that of itself it generates enthusiasm, inspiration, love. Our aim is that the understanding of humanity that enters our heads should saturate our actions and feelings as well. Real science is not just the dead knowledge so often taught today, but a knowledge that fills a person with love for the subject of that knowledge.

Thus, this understanding of humanity is brought to the teachers, in the seminar they are now taking to prepare themselves to educate your children. This understanding of humanity, this understanding of the growing child, should so saturate the teachers that a love of humanity enters the teaching. As recompense for the love that the teachers provide the children, a power will come forth, will well up from the children, that gives them the ability to take in more easily the material to be learned. The right kind of love, not overly protective love, but the real love that flows through what we do in the classroom or other teaching activities, determines whether the child will learn with ease or difficulty, whether the child's education is good or bad.

The third thing that we want to bring to the child and for which we prepare our teachers so that they understand the proper way to present it to the children, is willpower. We want to cultivate this willpower by allowing the child to do something artistic at a relatively early stage of childhood. Most people do not know the secret connection between the will and working in the proper way in childhood with drawing, painting, music and the other arts. We do so much good when the child has this opportunity.

Our children will learn to read and write from life itself. This is our intention. We will not pedantically force them to write letters that for every child at first seem all the same. They need not learn it as an abstract thing, as letters were for the North American Indians when the Europeans came. It is true, isn't it? The Europeans destroyed the North American Indians down to the root. One of the last chiefs of the North American Indian tribes destroyed by the Europeans tells that the white man, the paleface, came to put the dark man and all he stood for under the earth. "The dark man had certain advantages over the palefaces," the chief then continued; "he did not have the little devils on paper." We want to say that everything teachers pedantically and narrow-mindedly draw on the blackboard for the pupils to copy is seen as little devils by today's children. We can draw all such things from life. If we succeed in what we are attempting, the children will learn to read and write more quickly. When we derive everything from life, when writing comes from drawing and not from arbitrariness, children will learn more quickly. At the same time, we can raise strong-willed people who later in life will be up to the task.

We will not simply superficially say, "We want to educate people." In a profound manner, we first ask ourselves, modestly and honestly, "What is the Being of Humanity, and how does it appear in the developing Human Being?" We do not first go and ask political and industrial leaders, "How should we teach and educate people so that they can take their place in society?" We also do not ask, "What does this or that governmental body compel us to teach so that people can fulfill what the state demands of them?" No, we turn our questions to the uniform nature of humanity and its requirements. Yes, you see, in this respect the old social conditions are in conflict with what is necessary for a more socially oriented human future.

Today the state takes over the developing person, the child, at a particular age. The state would take over the child earlier, but the child is not clean enough for it. For a while, it leaves the rearing of and caring for the child to the parents. When the child has grown enough that it is no longer so dirty, the state takes over and dictates what we are to funnel into the child. Of course, the state allows us to funnel into the child only what is necessary for the workplace, thereby enabling itself to do with people as it will. Even when they are adults, people are often quite satisfied. The state tells them, "You will be assured of a lifelong job, and when you are no longer able to work, you will have a pension." Retirement is a notion that some circles of leading people treat as an ideal. They expect it from the state education. These people also expect that the state, through the religion teachers, will take their souls in hand so that these souls need not work, since the churches will do the work for them. They expect that the churches will, so to speak, provide a "soul retirement" after death. Today everyone wants to have everything done for them. This is the result of a totally false education.

A real education takes care that body, soul and spirit will be intrinsically free and independent. A real education takes care to put people into life. Do you believe that if we really ask people how we should bring them up, that is, if we inquire into the nature and being of humanity, we would then create impractical people? No, just the opposite! We are educating people who can, in truth, put themselves powerfully into life. In grammar school we are educating humans who, in later life, will know more of what is necessary for the outward, practical life. These people will have learned to think; these people will have learned to correctly feel; and these people will have learned to properly use their will. We want to introduce all of this, so that truth and strength can rule, not so that in pedagogy the phrase holds, "We should bring up children correctly." We should instead make the child a true person!

Much must happen in the outside world to create better social conditions. Much must happen in just the area where the Waldorf School wants to set a foundation stone for this great building. It would be something beautiful for you to say with heartfelt meaning, "We want to be pioneers for a future educational system. We want to be pioneers in the sense that we want to be the first to entrust our children to such an educational system of the future, one working for a new social life. We want to be pioneers in the sense that we do not believe that a few external changes will lead to a better social condition, but that a change must occur at the heart of science, art and education to bring about the desired condition of humanity."

How do people today often imagine what should actually happen? Socialization should occur, but most people, even those who quite honestly speak of socialization, think, "Sure, somewhere there are the universities, and they have already done everything right. It may be that we need to change the outward position of the university professors a little, but science itself, we may not change that in any way." Middle school, high school, trade school—people just do not think that outward life has come from these schools. But the people educated in these schools have created the outer life. At most, we think we should organize the lower level of education somewhat differently than it is now. This results in self-deception, in that we say, "We must provide education without cost." I would like to know how we can, in fact, do this. We just deceive ourselves, since we must pay for education. It cannot be free of cost—that is only "possible" through the deception of taxes or such things. We make up such phrases, which do not have any basis in reality.

People think that we should change this or that in the organization a little. We must subject everything to fundamental change, from top to bottom. We need another teacher training, another spirit in the school, even another love, different from that which modern sophisticated faculties bring into the schools. Unfortunately, all too few people think about that. You will perform a great service to humanity if you are pioneers in this respect, if you think we must renew the educational system for the betterment of humanity, and if you take part in this renewal with heartfelt interest and heartfelt sense. The more you think of taking part, of interesting yourselves in what is to happen in the Waldorf School, the better the faculty will succeed in working in unity with you for the betterment and blessing of your children, and thus for the whole of future humanity—at least within the boundaries that we can envision now.

People can work out ideals alone and write them down. The ideals can be beautiful and can please this or that person. Yes, people can think abstract ideals alone. But, with ideals that we should put into practice, such as the ideal of our new educational system, we are dependent upon finding understanding in the world. We want especially the parents of the children to be entrusted to the Waldorf School to be understanding of its ideal.

Mr. Molt has spoken of his responsibility, and he is right. This responsibility, though, is something that goes much further. We are all conscious of this responsibility as we prepare for the Waldorf School, and we will always remain conscious of it. Such a responsibility is always before us, when we work toward an ideal as radical as that of the Waldorf School. By taking up this ideal, we are forced to break with prejudices in the broadest sense. Truly, today it is not easy to find out everything we must do to educate children properly, particularly in grammar school. The empty phrase has caused such great havoc.

"We should teach the children through play." This is particularly the ideal of middle-class mothers who, through a certain kind of love—we might call it a doting affection—are devoted to their children. From one side we may emphasize, with a certain right, that education should not become drudgery for the child. We could take the position that we should "playfully" carry out education. We are all quite clear that in education we must bring play as well as work together in the proper relationship to prepare for life. However, we are also conscious that play which trains the child like an animal is play no longer. This play, often found in our schools today, trains the children like animals, just as before we pedantically drilled them. Play can only occur in freedom. However, play must alternate with another kind of activity so that children learn the seriousness of work, so that they are up to the seriousness of work in life. We will not work with empty phrases. We will have a time for work and a time for play. We will judge everything by the manifestations of the nature of the developing person, of the child.

Just as we should familiarize ourselves with the true understanding of humanity, so must we gradually bring the school to the point that the children happily go to it, that they are glad to go to this school. We will not seek to attain anything unnatural. It would be unnatural to believe that children, who should have vacation, should go to school and not play during vacation. We will also not be so foolish as to believe that children, after they have played for weeks, should sit well-behaved in the classroom upon just returning to school. We will understand our children. However, after awhile, through the way that we relate to the children, they will do their work during school time just as happily as they play during vacation. An ideal of the Waldorf School is that the children do what they should do, out of an inner force. We do not see our goal as simply to command the children. Rather, our goal is to relate to the children so that from our attitude the children feel, "I am glad to do this, I am happy to go through this with my teacher."

When your children come home from school, we hope that you enjoy it when they talk about the things they enjoyed at school. We hope that you enjoy the joyous faces of the children when they come home after school. We do not hope this because we want to make life into some sort of entertainment, but because we know how many of today's terrible social conditions result from something that could be different. We know that worse will come to humanity if we do not work for new social circumstances through conscientious new beginnings in education. We do everything possible to form education and upbringing as I have described it to you, not to do the child a favor, but because we know the power that joy gives to the child.

We want to create this new school as an example—this school so many people hunger for, but do not have the courage to look in the eye. We will have to believe, we will have to understand, that the so-called social question also rests upon the problem of education as I characterized it here, and that we can accomplish social change only in the way that we are attempting in the Waldorf School. It would be a great tragedy if the social impulse that is the foundation of the Waldorf School were ignored. May it first be recognized by those who entrust their children to the Waldorf School. We are all conscious of the responsibility of placing something in the world to which you should entrust the development and future of your children, come what may. We have not taken on the responsibility of what should happen here out of some sort of whim, but out of the recognition that such tasks are necessary in our time and that it is now particularly necessary to come to the developing human being, the child, with the best that humanity can understand.

I do not know if you know exactly the feeling of having gone through the world during these terrible war years, the last four or five years, and having seen how the children, the six- to nine-year-olds or still younger, have grown up. At times, you could feel quite a deep pain if you did not live unconsciously and thoughtlessly in the world, but lived, rather, with a consciousness of what lies ahead if we do not conceive some help for what has brought humanity to such a terrible state. You get a heavy heart, seeing the growing children lately. You cannot see them without having a deep heartache, if you do not decide at the same time, as far as you are able, to effect another way of bringing up children—a way that is different from the way people of today had to go, the way that has caused so much of the present unhappiness and misery. In the foremost sense, we create a piece of human future with education. We must be clear that we must relearn, must rethink, many things. Today, we experience many curious things from teachers in the upper and lower grades.

I recently spoke in a neighboring city that has a university. I said that, among other things, the social question also involves the fact that people, although depressed by questions about the organization of life, do not consider themselves to be in an inhumane condition. I expanded upon that further. Afterward—it is hard to believe that today such people still exist—a university professor came up and said he could not understand why an inhumane existence of the modern blue-collar worker was connected with the wage scale. He saw their situation as no different from that of, for instance, Caruso, who sings, and receives a payment of thirty to forty thousand marks for the evening. That would be just the same as when a blue-collar worker received his wages and as when he, as a professor, received his salary. He could see no difference. There would be only a difference in the size of the payment, but no essential difference. Therefore he could not see wages as being a degradation of human existence. Wages are wages.

That is the response we receive today from a highly educated teacher. We receive such responses also from teachers at lower schools. This only emphasizes the necessity for a renewal of our training and educational system. We can say, "Truly, today, when we hear what people around many higher schools say about a reformation of our social conditions, and about the necessity to reform the schools, that is the most vivid proof that we must reform these schools. These people can only say what they say because these schools have a form that we must change."

Now, two things could happen. Mr. Molt has had the ideal to found the school which today and over the next eight days shall be ceremoniously opened. Due to the peculiar circumstances of our time, people could misunderstand his intention. Resistance could arise so that we could not put this ideal into practice, and it would disintegrate after a short time. Then we would say, "Yes, Mr. Molt wanted something quite ideal, but it was utopian. No one can put something like that into practice so easily." Why is it utopian? It is utopian because it is not understood, or because it is resisted!

A second thing could happen. Understanding could arise for what is born out of true social understanding, understanding for the real practicality of this wish. Then what is desired will become customary. It will become so familiar, that at first you, and later others, will say, "There was someone who saw more practically than others who thought they knew all about practical life." People will not say, "This was utopian." People will say, "Something really practical was put into the world!"

May the second of these two possibilities come to pass! Those who have the heart and soul for the social development of humanity now and in the future see this as a necessity. We will be able to look with utmost satisfaction upon what will occur when you, the first to send your children to the Waldorf School, stand by the side of the teachers with understanding, with interest. That will be the beginning of what should thrive with this school, what can really prosper.

May it prosper! May it thrive, so that those who see this blossoming decide to do the same in many different places. Of course, only when, and may it be as soon as possible, the same takes place out of the same spirit in many places, only then can what should come out of the Waldorf School come out of it. Then soon many more will follow. The free spirit will rule and a free social training and educational system will spread over the civilized earth.

This spirit and this feeling will be instilled into the civilized earth and will be an important power for all that will help us to come to a better, more humane existence in social organization.

May we grasp that the social question is a manifold one, and that one of its most important aspects is the question of education. May understanding and vision arise in the hearts of many people and powers for thinking, feeling and willing arise in the children. Thus, these children, when they are grown, can look back thankfully to their parents, who stood and first saw the social question, but still suffered deprivation because they themselves could not be brought up within the new socially oriented education. To these parents who understand the idea of such an education, the children will look back thankfully. Those children will be carried into a new time, along with many others, by the power that has become theirs through a truly humane upbringing and a humane education.

People want to make children useful for life in many ways. The old teachers also said that. Through the new educational system and pedagogy, we want to put people more humanely into life. Through these children, raised in this way, life itself will be so formed that its humanness appeals to the decency of understanding people.

May this spirit rule in the founding of this work that Mr. Molt, through the Waldorf School, wants to give to a part of humanity.

Question Session Following the Lecture

Question: How will religious instruction be given in the Waldorf School? Also, how will the feelings of the children coming from other schools be taken into account?

Dr. Steiner: It must first be emphasized that, in the strictest sense, the Waldorf School does not teach a particular philosophy. We are not going to bring dogmatically to the children what we derive from a philosophy that has been stated here for years. We will use it only because we can use it to improve, to reform the instructional methods, the way of handling the instruction.

On the other hand, we must, because our modern time needs it, present the content of the child's religion. A Catholic teacher will instruct Catholic children in the Catholic tradition; a Catholic teacher will lead them in their religious exercises. The same is true for Protestant children. We do not seek to achieve the goals of the Waldorf School through the inculcation of any particular philosophy. What we want is that a new method of instructing and handling instruction, a new method of teaching and handling teaching arises out of what we do.

What happens to the children coming from other schools is a very important question, particularly for the older children. We will not begin with the first grade and then build upon that. Rather, we will begin with a complete elementary school. Thus, we will have children of all ages. Of course, through the methods we are now discussing in our seminar, we will later be able to do many things differently, when we have only children whom we taught beginning in the first grade. However, we will now take into account everything that the children have already learned. In each grade, we will begin with what the children have already learned and continue in the way appropriate to our methods. We will seek out only what is advantageous for the children without needing to repeat what they have already learned. In instructing, we can work very economically. Lay people have no idea of what we can accomplish. When we work so economically, we can teach in a quarter of an hour what normally takes two hours. This is a question of method; however, people must know the method. This is a very important thing, that we can teach in a quarter of an hour something that takes two hours to teach through incorrect methods. In that we use the right method, that is, a method that is in accord with human nature, we can teach more economically and accomplish much that other schools cannot accomplish, and still meet the criteria of the public school system. In this way, so long as we still have the present school system, when children graduate from our school, they can enter other schools without any loss of time. We will keep such things in mind.

4

Supersensible Knowledge
and Social Pedagogical Life

STUTTGART—SEPTEMBER 23, 1919

I N these serious times, we can look at what people who have considered the gravity of the situation think is necessary. We can see what new institutions they imagine are needed, what changes in our untenable conditions are necessary. If we do this, we will see people with the goodwill to dedicate themselves to new institutions, to cooperate in changing what seems to need change in one way or another. If we accept the responsibility for our all-too-obvious social circumstances, then we cannot get around the fact that, although there is so much goodwill and there are so many wonderful ideas, they collapse immediately or, in any event, are not carried out to the extent so necessary today.

Spiritual science seeks, through anthroposophical understanding, to open the path to supersensible knowledge for modern humanity. It has tried for decades to address the conspicuous problems of modern civilization, namely the flagging goodwill and the loss of the wonderful ideas that live in this goodwill. The spiritual science I have presented here for years has attempted to point out exactly what is so necessary in the present, and what so many modern people welcome with such great sympathy or reject with such great antipathy. It tries to point out, on the one hand, what has made conventional science so great, and, on the other hand, as we will discuss today, what this science lacks the means to understand, namely, human will and human feeling.

We live in a time when it is no longer possible for people simply to yield to their instinctive will impulses. The necessity to increasingly transform the old instinctive life into a fully conscious life is especially characteristic of our time, yet so many prejudices arise today when it comes to admitting this. That people must increasingly change the old instinctive motives of human nature into conscious motives is a historical fact, the most important historical fact. It is this fact that has led to the present crisis.

To this end, scientific advances over the last three or four centuries have done much for modern civilization. But today, anyone who contemplates the institutions that arise out of the most vital contemporary needs must come to feel the insufficiencies of modern times that come from the modern scientific orientation and way of thinking. Just now in this city a limited attempt is being made to solve a social problem, a social problem that is more important than most people want to believe. Perhaps this evening we can point out the difficulties of solving such a specific problem.

Through the insight into anthroposophical spiritual science that he has often demonstrated throughout the years, our friend Emil Molt has succeeded in founding the Free Waldorf School upon social thinking appropriate to our times. This school is intended for children of the workers at the Waldorf-Astoria factory and for a few others who will shortly be included. The imprint of modern society is visible in the manner of the school's creation and in its connection with an industrial firm. This school must take into account the most practical needs of the people who entrust it with the education of their children. We could say that it is symbolic that this school was created in connection, in direct connection, with the industrialism that gives rise to the most important social questions of our time.

In founding the school, the faculty (for whom I held an introductory seminar lasting several weeks) considered the social pedagogical tasks relevant to modern culture. More than we are aware, our picture of modern civilization (as I already mentioned) results from the way our imagination has developed out of our understanding of physical nature. As I have emphasized for decades, spiritual science fully recognizes the value and meaning of the modern scientific way of thinking; in fact, spiritual science values conventional science more highly than that science values itself. Nevertheless, because conventional science so colors our picture of modern civilization, spiritual science must go beyond it. I have also emphasized that the means used by spiritual science to come to its understanding of the world differ from those of conventional science. I have repeatedly explained how we can really enter into the supersensible world through the path of spiritual science, how, through the development of inner capacities that otherwise only sleep in human nature, the way opens for us to see into the spiritual world in which we live. We can see into the spiritual world just as we can recognize the laws of the physical world through our senses, through reason, through associated events. I have explained how we, by awakening dormant capabilities, can look into the spiritual world that always surrounds us, but is unknown to us because the necessary sense organs remain undeveloped in ordinary life.

Today I want to discuss the capacities that spiritual science uses to see into the supersensible world—healthy, quite normal capacities of human nature. Those who want a deeper insight into how spiritual science works need not concern themselves with the accusations of our critics that it is based upon the use of unwholesome powers. It is quite simple to show the source of Anthroposophy and its path to the supersensible world.

If you look at my book *How To Know Higher Worlds,* you will see that I describe those stages of supersensible knowledge that people can attain through the development of certain capacities sleeping within them: 1) the Imaginative stage of knowledge, 2) the stage of Inspiration and 3) the stage of true Intuition. Now, where does spiritual science find the forces involved in such things as Imagination, Inspiration and Intuition? We can show that certain capacities forming the basis of human nature are at work during childhood. Later in life, when people have reached their normal size, when growth is complete, in a sense these forces lie unused. This spring I discussed the various stages of child development.[1] I remarked that during the first period of life, people are primarily imitative beings. They instinctively learn everything that people around them do, and they imitate this in their movements, sounds, speech, even in their thoughts. This imitative behavior continues until approximately the change of teeth, until approximately seven years of age. Then those who can more exactly observe human nature begin to see another activity. They can observe the need in human nature, beginning at six or seven years of age and continuing until sexual maturity, to rely upon people with experience, upon those adults in whom children can devotedly believe. During this period, children need to act under the influence of honored authorities. The self-reliance that is based in people's confidence in their power of judgment, the self-reliance that enables them to involve themselves in all sorts of things in life, first appears with sexual

---

1. Translators' note: Lectures of 5/11/19, 5/18/19, 6/1/19, contained in *A Social Basis for Primary and Secondary Education* (GA 192), Waldorf Institute, Adelphi University, New York, 1975.

maturity at the age of fourteen and continues to develop until the age of twenty or twenty-one.

These are three quite distinct periods of human youth. Only people who have lost healthy judgment due to all kinds of prejudices can overlook what develops in the child, what causes physical development until the age of seven when bodily development is relatively complete—the form continues to grow but the general structure is complete. Only such people can overlook how those forces that act formatively until seven years of age subsequently work more inwardly, particularly as inner growth. They act as living forces, making children stronger until fourteen years of age. They work between the ages of fourteen and twenty to strengthen those organs directed toward the environment, those organs that are capable of immersing themselves in their surroundings. In this time those inner spiritual forces act upon the human physical body. Inner spiritual forces act in quite differing ways upon the human body until seven, then fourteen, then twenty-one years of age. Forces that for an unprejudiced observer are quite clearly inner spiritual forces work on human organs to master them and develop them further.

These forces really exist. The forces that in a certain sense cause the crystallization of the second set of teeth out of human nature, a meaningful conclusion to the stage of human development ending at age seven, really exist. The forces that work mysteriously on that part of human beings that is connected with growth and the unfolding of human nature until age fourteen really exist. These forces are real; they are active. But after the completion of physical development (around the age of twenty), where are these inner spiritual forces that have acted upon our physical form? They still exist; they are still there. These inner forces fall asleep, just as the forces we use in our everyday life, our everyday work from waking to sleeping, fall asleep and become dormant while we sleep. The forces of human nature that blazed during childhood and youth, the forces that fired the developmental changes that transform children into adults, and everything connected with these changes, fall asleep around the age of twenty. Those who look at the whole human being know that at the very moment when human beings reach this point, the forces that acted in the child, in the youth, step back into the innermost part of human nature. These forces go to sleep.

We can awaken the forces that have brought forth the processes normally observed between the ages of fourteen and twenty, through which we slowly gain an understanding of our surroundings, through which those organs develop that can form only after puberty. These organs are not one-sidedly oriented toward sexual love, but are formed such that we can deepen our love of all humanity. This loving absorption in all humanity gives us true understanding of the world. The forces we use until the age of twenty-one for growing and forming the inner organs become inflexible, just critical intellect. A certain inner spiritual force stops working formatively. It becomes an imaginary inner force, a power of the soul, no longer so strong as it was earlier when it had to guide human formation. If we can find it sleeping in human nature, this power that once was a formative force but after the age of twenty no longer is, if we develop it so it exists with the same strength as before, then, acting now through love, it becomes Imaginative power. People attain a capacity to see the world not only through abstract concepts, but in pictures that are alive, just as dreams are alive, and that represent reality just as our abstract concepts do. The same force that previously acted upon the healthy developing human to form the capacity to love, can enable us to see such pictures of the world and to reach the first stage of supersensible knowledge. We can awaken this human capacity and plunge it deeper into our surroundings than normal thinking and normal sensing can go.

Then we can go further, since the forces that cause the important formative changes from approximately seven years of age, from the change of teeth, until sexual maturity, are also sleeping in us. These forces sleep deeper under the surface of normal soul life than the forces I just characterized as Imaginative. When we reawaken these idle formative capacities, when we call these spiritual powers out of their sleep, they become the forces of Inspiration. These teach us that Imaginative pictures are filled with spiritual content, that these pictures, which appear to be dreams but really are not, reflect a spiritual reality that exists in our surroundings, outside ourselves.

We can go even deeper, into the strongest forces sleeping in human nature, those that have worked upon human formation from birth until the change of teeth. These formative forces that were active in the first years of life have withdrawn themselves most deeply from external life. If we bring them forth again in later life and imbue them with Imagination and Inspiration, we will then have the Intuitive powers of supersensible knowledge. These are the powers that enable us to delve into the reality of the spiritual world in the same way that we can delve into the physical world through the senses and the will usually associated with the body.

In three stages, through Imagination, Inspiration and Intuition, we gain access to the supersensible world. These powers do not employ anything abnormal, but actually are the most normal of all things, namely the forces of healthy human development from birth until the early twenties. These forces then lie fallow, but we can bring them forth again. When they are no longer occupied with forming us, we can use them to open up the spiritual world.

I have now given you some idea of the source of those forces that open the way for spiritual science to enter the supersensible world. Those who seriously wish to follow this path will know how to differentiate what it can properly give from what simple conventional science, simple scientific understanding, can offer. Why do I continually emphasize modern scientific understanding? It would not be so necessary to emphasize this scientific understanding and the attitude that derives from it, if modern popular thinking, including social thinking and social policies, were not so completely patterned after it. To be sure, we have here something that many people seldom consider. However, we must consider it if we wish to find something that will really lead to healing our ailing social conditions. We must be clear that scientific thinking so completely permeates all human thinking that when people begin to consider something else, they automatically revert to the modern scientific attitude and manner of thinking.

What is, in fact, the social political thinking of the second half of the nineteenth century right up to the present? What is it that fundamentally, even now, is presented to us as socialist theory? It is a social thinking patterned after mechanistic scientific thinking. Why does this social thinking appear to be so unfruitful, as I have often described it in these lectures? Because this social thinking, take for example the Marxist English Socialist thinking, is infested through and through with a conventional scientific attitude, an attitude that when used in this area simply cannot accomplish anything.

Now look at the most important characteristic of what I have referred to today as supersensible understanding in the sense of spiritual science. The most important characteristic is that this supersensible understanding uses those forces closely connected with what is human. What forces more closely connected with human nature could we possibly use than those that form human nature itself? How could we possibly use anything more human to achieve an ideal, to achieve anything we want to accomplish? How could we use forces for cognition more human than those that we can bring out of hiding the moment they are no longer needed to form human nature? There is a way of understanding in contrast to the modern scientific attitude and socio-political way of thinking, a life of abstract concepts connected only with the structure and function of the human head. This way of understanding is through those forces that people still retain after their formation is complete at the age of twenty or so. This way of understanding uses forces allowed to sleep, but which are more real because they work on human formation. What we can obtain from scientific concepts and happily use in the social sciences, and wish to use in social pedagogical tasks—these concepts and ideas, in fact, everything that we can obtain in this way for our souls, are only a reflection of reality in comparison to the content of supersensible knowledge. Every concept we can gain when our reason combines sense impressions and observations, everything that we know from our will impulses—all this is actually only a shadow, a reflection, in contrast to what is so tightly enmeshed with human growth and activity and existence as the forces that form us. Thus, the abstract character (the character of being "independent of human nature") arises out of the scientific way of thinking that does not require people to use their will. We are proud of obtaining such knowledge that we can refer to as scientific and can call "objective."

Concerning knowledge, spiritual science does not attempt to throw what is human out, but rather to draw it into the world. It attempts to come to its knowledge through just those forces that form people. We can observe that scientific concepts, and socio-political concepts patterned after the same methods, satisfy human intellectual curiosity. They satisfy the intellect, but clearly do not have the power to enliven, to infuse, to ignite human will. Were this scientific viewpoint and its one-sidedness to become increasingly stronger and continually more dominant, in the end human willpower would completely atrophy. Nowadays we must motivate human willpower, atrophying under the influence of the scientific mentality, with something that can ignite it. This ability to stimulate willpower arises from people themselves because it can be drawn out of human nature as spiritual scientific knowledge.

This is what spiritual science wants to do, and what spiritual science, as we mean it here, can do. It wants to effect an understanding that is not simply there for the intellect alone, but flows into the feeling and the will.

Today, particularly in education, people repeatedly insist that we should not teach children knowledge simply for the sake of knowledge, that we should also teach them to be capable, to be able to work; we should develop the will. Here we have one of those points where the goodwill of our contemporaries becomes evident. Certainly much goodwill exists when people today say that we should not simply have "knowledge schools," but schools that develop a capacity to work, schools that develop capabilities. But goodwill alone does not suffice. We need the capacity to illuminate this goodwill, to brighten it with true insight. We do not achieve this insight, however, by simply saying that we should create "schools of capabilities" instead of "schools of knowledge." The core of this insight is that now we must move more and more from the instinctive to the conscious. It is necessary not only to affect the will instinctively, not only that the teacher instinctively affect the pupil. The important thing is that concepts, ideas and imagination be allowed to flow from the teacher to the child. However, these must be concepts that are not simply concepts in thought, but concepts that can stimulate the will, that can satisfy the whole person. We are not concerned that people often stress that only the will should be developed, or only the feeling. No, what we are concerned with is that we gain the possibility of working to obtain such an insight, such concepts that have the power in themselves to go into the will, to develop the inner fire of the will. This is what we need today to heal the present mentality, to properly use the will in the second social pedagogical area.

The first social pedagogical area is what the recently founded Waldorf School is intended to serve, namely that area encompassing the elementary grades.[2] Elementary education should prepare people for true social thinking today and in the near future. We shall see how much this is a question of spiritual science, a question of the path into supersensible worlds.

The other aspect of the social pedagogical question is to prepare people to learn from life. We do not fare well in life if we view it as a rigid and foreign object. We can place ourselves correctly in life only when every moment, every day, every week, every year becomes a source of learning for our further development. Regardless of how far we go in our schooling, we will have accomplished the most if, through this schooling, we have learned how to learn from life. If we find the proper way to place ourselves in relationship to everyone we meet, then they will become for us a source of further development through everything they are and through everything they consciously and unconsciously give us. In everything that we do, hour by hour, day by day, week by week, we experience ourselves such that everything we experience in our surroundings becomes a source of continuing further development. Life is a school for every healthy person.

---

2. Translators' note: In the Germany of 1919, many children finished formal schooling with the eighth grade and then entered an apprenticeship.

However, neither of these social pedagogical realms, learning in school or learning from life, can meet the needs of society now and in the near future if they are not strengthened by what spiritual science can provide.

Today, people think we should educate children as "individuals." We also find other fundamental thoughts represented in modern education. With one exception, I do not wish to go into the details of modern pedagogy. However, I do wish to mention that this pedagogy contains certain standards that are made clear to those who teach. The teachers are to educate according to these standards. Much goodwill lives in these standards also. People have done an exceptional amount of well-meant thinking in forming this pedagogy. However, what is necessary now and in the near future is a *living* pedagogy. What we need is a *living* pedagogy, derived from supersensible human understanding, that replaces an abstract pedagogy that sets up standards for teaching children.

This supersensible perception of human beings does not at all ignore sense-perceptible understanding—it takes it fully into account. The sense-perceptible view of human beings, with all its understanding of anatomy, physiology, and so forth, treats people as an abstraction. Supersensible perception adds the spirit-soul element, while at the same time taking sense-perceptible knowledge fully into account. It observes the *whole* person, with emphasis upon the *development* of the whole person. It can, therefore, concentrate upon the developing whole person at the time when the parents entrust him or her to the elementary school at about the age of seven. What developed in the child as a result of imitation requires the support of authority during this life-forming period. Only when we are able to look at people in such a way, can we see what truly lives in them. In that we observe such a change, we can see what is unfolding in people. If you notice in the right way, with sensitivity, what wants to develop in people at six or seven years of age, and if you have not *become* a teacher, but *are* a teacher, then an awareness for this most wonderful riddle awakens through the innermost living forces without the necessity of pedagogical standards—the developing person continuously offers him- or herself to your soul's eye.

Here lies something that a true social pedagogical reformation, which must be the basis of a modern unified elementary school, must really take into account. Here we must say that it is essentially unimportant whether new teachers have really learned what is often taught as pedagogy, as special methods. What is important for future teachers is that, through their training, they have become capable of looking into the developing person. What is important is that they have acquired the skills that they can acquire through a thorough, real understanding of human beings. What is important is that they have become capable in the presence of each child and in each moment to *newly form and re-form* the educational task.

For the true teacher, pedagogy must be something living, something new at each moment. Everything that teachers carry in their souls as memories robs them of their originality. New insights into the nature of developing humans that allow the pedagogy to change and be alive in those people who teach must replace pedagogical norms. We could even say that the best pedagogy (stated radically) is one that the teacher continually forgets and that is continually reignited each time the teacher is in the presence of the children and sees in them the living powers of developing human nature. When an all-encompassing interest in the secrets of the world, in the enigma of the world and in world views accompanies such an attitude, then within the teachers will live what enables them to give that part of themselves that should enter the being of the children.

How can the teacher's inner nature become so alive in the way I have just described it? Certainly no longer through a way of thinking derived from science, but only when the teacher's will is ignited through a science drawn from forces connected with human nature. The teachers who have absorbed what spiritual science knows about the supersensible nature of human beings, who have inwardly enlivened this, who in a living fashion carry within themselves a science founded upon those forces through which the child is to be educated—such teachers can make this knowledge into a living inner fire for teaching. The basis of such a pedagogical art is supersensible knowledge, that is, the same forces that from day to day, from week to week, from year to year bring about the growth and development of the child.

Think about it for a moment. Consider how close the sources of pedagogical art are to what grows in the child when supersensible knowledge controls and directs what the teacher brings to the child! We should not search for new abstract ideas nor clever new rules in what we refer to as social pedagogical effectiveness. What we should search for is that *the living should replace the dead, the concrete should replace the abstract.*

To demand such things today is much more necessary than people often imagine. It is remarkable that people cannot imagine that there is supersensible knowledge that acts upon sensible knowledge, that acts upon life and teaching, upon know-how and capabilities. Already people have begun to misunderstand the core of the Waldorf School, and thus they slander, often unconsciously, what we intend with the Waldorf School. People think the Waldorf School must be some kind of parochial school because those who stand at its cradle begin with spiritual science. They think that it is a school that teaches Anthroposophy to the children. They do not have any idea how deeply stuck they are in old ideas when they assume this, whether it be with a positive or negative attitude. We have absolutely no need to assert Anthroposophy, to assert it as a point of view by developing anthroposophical concepts and seeing to it that children learn these as they previously learned religion. That is not at all our task. We will continue with what we have already stated, namely that the Protestant and Catholic religion teachers shall teach the Protestant and Catholic religions. We will not set any obstacles in the way of the desire to give this religious instruction. We will keep our promises in this regard. We do not seek in any way to bring any new philosophical opinions into the school. We seek something else. Our viewpoint will result from spiritual science because it comes from human nature. We will pay attention to the way it develops human know-how, human capabilities, the way it directly flows into the human will. Our task lies in our pedagogical activities: how we act in a school, how we teach, how we plan the lesson and its goals, which teaching methods to use, how knowledge and philosophy affect the skill and capability of the teacher. These are our tasks.

For this reason, we will have to correct much that (out of goodwill, but without the necessary insight) people consider to be the goals and content of modern educational activity. For instance, people often say that we should emphasize visual aids.[3] Yes, certainly, within boundaries, it is good to use illustrative material, that is, to teach children about things that we show them directly. But, we must not allow these materials to lead to a slide into the banality and triviality of superficial consideration. People always want to stoop to the level of the

---

3. Translators' note: The reader should be aware that the "visual aids" and "illustrative materials" meant here are to be understood as actual materials in the classroom, as distinct from a verbal or written description of the object of discussion. Prior to this time illustrative material was rarely used in the classroom, and it was a somewhat controversial innovation in 1919.

child, and then all kinds of trivialities result, like those we find when we read visual aid guides. We concerned ourselves with such things while forming the Waldorf School. There we could see how trivial the so-called visual aids are that are derived completely out of the materialistic attitude of our time. We could see how forced instruction is when the teacher stoops to the child's level of understanding, when the teacher is not to teach the child anything other than what the child can easily comprehend.

Now, if you only teach children what they can understand, then you neglect what can be the most beautiful thing in human life. If you always want to stoop to the level of what the children can already comprehend, then you do not know what it means later in life, perhaps at the age of thirty or thirty-five, to look back upon what you were taught in school. You do not understand what it means to have been taught something that you did not fully comprehend because you were not yet mature enough. But it comes up again. Now you notice that you are more mature, because you now understand it. Such a re-living of what has been taught forms the real connection between the time in school and the whole rest of life. It is immensely valuable to hear much in school that we cannot fully comprehend until we re-experience it later in life. We rob the children of this possibility when, with banal instruction, we stoop to the level of the child's understanding.

What then is the task of the teacher who wants to bring the children something they can absorb, but perhaps will understand only after many decades? Teachers must have the necessary inner life forces so that through their personality, through what they put into the teaching, they can give the children something they cannot yet fully understand. A relationship exists between the teacher and the children through which the teacher can bring things to the children. Things can be brought to the children through the way in which they live in the teacher, because the children feel the desire to experience the world that is aglow within the teacher. That is why the children can grasp them. It is tremendously important that the teachers become leaders in this way, that through the fire that lives in them, they become a wellspring for what the children will carry in their own lives. Compare this with how the banal instruction children receive dims with time.

There are many other examples to show that pedagogy must be something living, something stirred up in the teachers out of an understanding of human beings obtained through human capacities. More than anyone else, the teacher needs an understanding of humanity based upon a supersensible view of human beings. If, in teaching, we would use what comes from a supersensible world view and understanding of humanity, we could immediately remove all abstractions so that the teaching would come from the practical.

There are people today who think that they are practical, who think that they stand in practical life, but it is their "practicality," which is really only routine, that caused the terrible misery and misfortune that resulted in the war, and in which we still find ourselves today. Instead of obtaining an insight into what supersensible knowledge could achieve for education, these people say supersensible knowledge has nothing to do with the true practicalities of life. They have conjured up these miserable times because they have always said this, because, in reproachable carelessness, they have thrown out the true supersensible content of practical life. We have scarcely caught our breath, and now these people want to continue this stupid practice by kicking to death every truly earnest desire for improvement. If those people who absolutely do not want to see what is necessary for our time are again victorious, then in a short time we will again have the same misery that started in

1914. Those people who wish to crush everything supersensible in the activities they so slander, which are in reality so practical, are exactly those people who have led us into this misery. That is what we need to see clearly today.

I would not have spoken these serious words had not the terrible croakings of doom again arisen where we want to create something quite practical, like the Waldorf School. We should have learned something from the terrible events of the last four to five years, and we should progress. We must keep a sharp eye on those who do not want to progress, who want to begin again where they left off in 1914. We need not worry that they will keep a sharp eye on us—that they will do for sure. But, we must also keep a sharp eye on them. All people must unite who have a sense that something must happen today that, on the one hand, really originates out of the true spirit, and, on the other hand, is capable of affecting serious practical life.

For such very practical reasons, what is often an empty slogan, particularly concerning pedagogical questions, must for once be handled with objective seriousness. We must take into account, for instance (we paid particular attention to such things in the seminar for the Waldorf School faculty), that around nine years of age something important ends and something new begins with children. Until the age of nine, children are strongly entwined with their surroundings. The imitative principle is still enmeshed in the authoritative principle. The possibility of developing the feeling of self first begins at the age of nine, so that, for instance, scientific facts, nature studies of the plant and animal world, can be brought to the child. At the same time, the stage between seven and nine years of age is such that we do well not to bring the children anything that is taught out of convention, that is not basic and does not obviously flow out of human nature.

We must *gradually* lead children into reading and writing. Anyone can see that the letters we have today are something conventional. (With Egyptian hieroglyphics, it was different.) That means we must teach writing starting from drawing. At first we do not pay any attention to the shapes of the letters, but draw forms. We must begin basic drawing and painting, along with music, in the lowest grades. We must derive the whole education from the child's artistic capabilities. The children's artistic capabilities touch their entire being. They touch the child's will and feeling, and then, through will and feeling, the intellect. We then go on. We continue with drawing and painting to motivate the will through artistic instruction. We go on to writing and develop letters out of the drawn forms. Only then comes reading—it is even more intellectual than writing. We develop reading out of writing. I am giving these details so you can see that spiritual science is not off in the clouds but enters into all details of practical instruction. A living understanding of humanity, which must replace an abstract pedagogy, leads into all the details, into the ways in which we teach mathematics, writing, and languages.

So much for the special area of instructional pedagogy.

The social aspect of pedagogy encompasses all of practical living. After we have finished school, we go out into "real life," but our conventional education creates a gulf between us and life. Thus we see that there is something instinctive in the great questions of humanity. Although these questions address the needs of life, there is no insight for solving them.

I would like to take note of another question that has concerned modern civilization for some time, the so-called feminist question, namely, what forms the gulf between men and women. People are correct in trying to close this gap, but they cannot close it when they do not really understand what is *common* between men and women. If they only pay attention to what they can learn about human beings in the physical world and from the modern scientific way of thinking, the difference between men and women remains extreme. We will first bridge the abyss between men and women when we bring the differences in perception and ways of working in the world into balance. We will attain this balance through what we can arrive at through the knowledge, will and feeling that exist in the forces that form the basis of human nature. What men do not have, but women do, gives men a certain inclination; and what women do not have, but men do, gives women a certain inclination. During the time when people are physically female, they are spiritually male, and during the time they are physically male, they are spiritually female. If what can come into our society from spiritual science would permeate our culture, then the ground would be prepared for such things as the so-called feminist question. We can apply this to numerous questions, but I only want to remark about one other.

People cry out for organization. It is obvious that they cry out for it since the complicated relationships of modern social life require organization. I have said much in my lectures about the nature of such structure. However, people think that we need only to organize things according to current scientific principles, according to modern socio-political thinking, without spiritual science. Lenin and Trotsky organize, Lunatscharsky organizes according to these principles. They have placed economic life into a mechanistic form, and they want to do the same with spiritual life. Neither the stories of various people who judge out of their impressions, nor what journalists and other people who have recently been in Russia tell, is important. What we can use are Lenin's writings. They show anyone with insight what to expect: the organizational death of everything that is a true source of humanity, of what lies in the individual human being and in human nature. No greater foe of true human progress exists than what is now happening in the East.

Why is this? Because they absolutely ignore what can come from spiritual development, namely true social pedagogical life forces. We must organize, but we must be conscious that although we want to organize, people must live in this organization. People must live in this organization and have the opportunity to teach what the inner source of human nature is, what is hidden after people have grown, what we can again bring out of the sleeping powers of their human nature. Not everyone needs to be a clairvoyant and experience what can be experienced through the awakened powers of human nature, but everyone can be *interested* in what humanity can achieve through these living human forces.

When people take interest in such things, then a new capability awakens in them. This is a capability we can best characterize when we bring to mind an area where people already have somewhat weakened sensibilities. This capability can be likened to what a language is to all the people connected by it. To discover the spirit living in the language, those who speak *one* language must first understand the genius, the wonderful artistic structure of the language, even though they already speak it. They need to understand the spirit emanating from the language that permeates the people and forms the language into a unified whole. In that we learn to speak, we absorb, not consciously, but instinctively and unconsciously, with every word and with every connotation, something that reveals to us the genius of the language in a mysterious way. Social life is something that lives in many instincts. Language has always been one of the most wonderful social instruments. Only, in modern times, as we go from East to West, language has become increasingly abstract. People feel less and less what the sounds of the language say to the heart and to the head, and particularly the connections that the language forms to speak to the heart and to the head. People feel less and less the mysterious way in which the genius of the language makes impressions upon them.

Many other things that touch people as does the genius of language will become effective if a general human development becomes more widespread through the activity of the elementary school—acting not as a parochial school, but through rationally formed instruction. Then when people meet one another, they can unite through speech. Every conversation, every relationship to another person, becomes a source for the further development of our soul. What we do in the world that affects other people becomes a source of our own further development. We can first develop the elements of communication between people if we meet other people with those feelings aroused in us. We can develop this communication if we do not follow abstract modern science, but take up the living fire within us. This living fire can come to us from a science that is connected to what in human nature allows people to grow until twenty years of age, and from then on can lead to a development of supersensible knowledge.

The school of life can follow formal schooling when those forces that make us students of life are ignited. We will meet people in one or another abstract organization, in a political or in an economic organization. We will feel a bond, and see that we are connected with them in a very special way. Alongside those connections formed out of external needs, intimate mysterious connections between one soul and another can form in the future if the results of true spiritual development live in human souls. Human experience will be that you have lived through something with a person in a previous earthly life, and now you meet again. Inner ties lying deep in our souls will form spiritual-soul connections out of external life in the cold, sober organizations that we do not really need.

Even though I have described the three forms of the social organism since spring, the spiritual sphere, the rights-political sphere and the economic sphere, I must emphasize that these are three external forms. Inside these three external forms will live the intimate inner connections forged from one human soul to another. People will recognize each other more clearly than they do today. If, in place of antisocial desires, those social motives that are the basis of true social life are present, then the modern scientific way of thinking can at last become fully useful for humanity. Through this scientific way of thinking we will be able to properly master the external lifeless nature that appears as technology and other things. The ethical, moral forces that can be kindled by the spiritual will derived from spiritual science will take care that the results of technology are useful to human beings. An inner structure that carries people and forms human life will come into the external forms of the social organism. Without this inner structure we cannot develop a fruitful external social form.

That is what I wanted to mention to you today, that spiritual science as we think of it here is not in any way abstract, is not something floating in the clouds, is not, as some people claim, metaphysical. It is something that streams directly into human will and makes people more adept and more capable of living. This remains unrecognized by those who refuse to see the present need for our spiritual science. They will also refuse to see that something like the Waldorf School has been formed, not arbitrarily, but out of truly practical life.

Can we expect much from those people setting the tone today? This spring and summer I repeatedly mentioned in my social lectures (I only mention this as characteristic of much of the modern intellectual attitude) that among the issues of the working class is that, in the future, work must not be a commodity. In a neighboring city I spoke about the "commodity character" of work. I think that people need only the tiniest bit of common sense to understand the general intent in the words "commodity character." This morning I received a newspaper published in that neighboring city. The lead editorial closes with the sentence, "I am confused by the sentence that 'work must be freed from its *true character*'." [4] Yes, that's possible today. Today it is possible for people who are unable to understand something so clearly related to modern culture as "commodity character" to make judgments about such things. Someone like this could not in an entire life have possibly heard of the "commodity character of human work." How do such people live in the present time? When it is possible to become so out of touch with reality, it is no wonder that we cannot get together in modern social life.

This is not only possible for people such as the writer of this editorial, it is also possible for those people who think they know everything about practical life. It is possible for people who, at every opportunity, look down upon what appears to them to be idealistic. They do not speak about real life any differently than people who see a U-shaped piece of iron and are told it is a magnet. "No," they answer, "this is used to shoe horses." These modern people who wish to shut supersensible knowledge out of practical life are like the person who sees a horseshoe-shaped magnet only as a horseshoe. They do not think anything can be true that does not directly meet their limited powers of understanding.

Today there are many more people than we think who hinder social progress. There are many people who do not want to understand that we cannot simply say that the last

---

4. Translator's note: Steiner used the German word *Warencharakter* (commodity character); the editor understood him to say *wahren Charakter* (true character). Their pronunciation is nearly identical.

four or five years have brought something terrible to the people of Europe—something more terrible than ever before existed in historical times. To this we must add that now things must occur out of a depth of thought that people have never before reached in the course of what we call history. We have come to a time in which people think completely abstractly. Most abstract are the political opinions and programs that existed at the beginning of the twentieth century and that grew out of a modern scientific education. People do not want to understand how abstract, how foreign are the means they wish to use to come to grips with life. People think that they are practical. For example, people see today that in world trade money runs through their fingers, that the German mark is worth less day by day. And from day to day we do exactly *those* things that, of course, cause the value of the mark to fall. "Practical" people have again taken the helm. So long as people do not see that truly practical life does not lie where they, in 1914, looked for it, but in the understanding of the ideals of life, so long will nothing get better. People today are not modest enough to admit that things will get better only if they come to a deepening in their *insight*. Goodwill will not do it alone, that is the cancer of our times. It will be necessary that people see more and more what the true basis of spiritual cognition is. Spiritual cognition, because it is based upon the development of the same powers that work in the formation of healthy human beings, can place them in social pedagogical life. What we need today is spirituality—not a naive spirituality, not a spirituality lost in the clouds, not a metaphysical spirituality, but true spirituality that affects practical life, true spirituality that can master the problems of life. We also need practical insight into life; we need to *be* in life, but in such a way that our view of life kindles a desire to bring this spirituality into life.

From a spiritual-scientific point of view, people must understand one thing, otherwise no progress will be possible in our unfortunate times. The axiom must be:

Seek the truly practical material life, but seek it such that it does not numb you to the Spirit working in it.

Seek the Spirit, but seek it not in supersensible lust, out of supersensible egotism; seek it because you want to become selfless in practical life, selfless in the material world.

Turn to the old maxim: Never Spirit without matter, never matter without Spirit!

Do this so that you can say, "We want to perform all material deeds in the light of the Spirit, and we want to seek the light of the Spirit in such a way that it develops warmth within us for our practical deeds."

Spirit brought by us to matter,
Matter wrought by us to its revelation
Driving the Spirit out;
Matter receiving from us Spirit revealed,
Spirit forged by us back into matter—
These create that Living Being,
Bringing humanity to true progress,
Progress only longed-for
By the best desires in the depths of human souls.

5

The Social Pedagogical Significance
of Spiritual Science

BASEL—NOVEMBER 25, 1919

A Public Lecture

I N the face of facts that speak loud and clear, we do not need
to prove that the social question is now one of the most burning public concerns. However, those who can observe these
facts without prejudice can also see that much deeper human
questions play into modern social demands than the problems
usually associated with slogans. If you look beyond current academic activity and trends to social facts, you can see how
deeper human questions in a certain respect spring from these
social problems.

It is obvious that, for the most part, academic life stands by
helplessly when confronted with these burning social demands.
I need only mention two things to prove this helplessness. We
know that in the course of recent cultural development, in
addition to the other branches of science, a theoretical socio- or
world economics has emerged. We know how the differing
schools of thought have affected the area of world economics in
the last centuries, particularly in the nineteenth century. We
know that there was a mercantilist school, a physiocratic school
and so forth, and we know how these different streams have
attempted to understand social facts. They have attempted to
discover how human social understanding can become a part of
human willing, for example, in various governmental programs. However, we have seen that these different theoretical

viewpoints have not resulted in any really thorough, fruitful social initiatives. The clearest proof of that is the form that world economic theory has taken. It has slowly withdrawn into a scientific observation of social life and world economics. It has withdrawn into a description of social facts.

Specifically, we see the newest efforts in this area developing into all manner of descriptions or statistical observations and such. However, we do not see anywhere an impulse that can really be carried into social will, that can be fruitful for the social activity of public life. The incapacity of world economic theories in this area is thus evident.

On the other hand, we see the growth of social ideas and social demands from a wide spectrum of the working class.

Certainly, we would have much to discuss if we wanted to speak about the historical development of these more-than-half-century-old social demands. Here we wish to take note of only *one* feature, of *one* characteristic of these demands. I wish to express it like this: There were also older efforts in this direction, efforts that did not simply rely upon theoretical contemplation, as has been done in world economics, but that were based upon the goals of people seeking a new social structure. Since the time of these efforts (we need only recall Fourier, Saint-Simon, Louis Blanc and so forth), a quite different element has entered into these contemplations. This can be characterized by a certain mistrust. Among the masses and their socialist leaders a certain antipathy is prevalent concerning everything that arises out of the spirit, out of contemplation, out of the human willing that should lead to a rejuvenation of social relationships.

Those whose feeling and thinking embody the intellectual impulses of modern times have much goodwill toward achieving social change. Regardless of that goodwill, the belief has arisen that all this has a utopian character. In spite of all the human inventiveness and goodwill, the belief has arisen that it is impossible to create impulses that will lead to practical changes in social life, to a truly practical reformation of social life. Disbelief in the human spirit and its social ideas has become the prevailing sentiment of the masses and their leaders.

Thus, something has come forth that people in these groups feel to be a foregone conclusion—so much a foregone conclusion that to fight against it is extraordinarily difficult. The conviction has arisen that *only* the means of economic production can stimulate a reformation. The conviction has arisen that, in a certain sense, the human will is powerless and must wait until the means of production themselves cause a different configuration in social life. It has become a habit to speak of everything created through thinking as an ideology, as something powerless in real life. It has also become habitual to speak as though only material relationships and changes are real, as though thinking emerges from these like a wisp of smoke. People speak of historical materialism because they see reality only in materialism, particularly in economic activity. People view what comes from the human spirit as something that rises like smoke out of what is real—in this case, economic activity—and forms a kind of ideological superstructure.

If we look at theoretical world economics, based as it is on the world view of conventional science, or at the thoughts of such thoroughly honest, creative personalities as Saint-Simon or Louis Blanc, whose work comes fully out of modern intellectual life, a question arises. We now ask, given what these two sides desire, is it so incomprehensible that a disbelief in true spiritual impulses has occurred?

No, it is not. If we look at the basic character of modern intellectual life we will find the main reason. The basic character of modern intellectual life has slowly become purely abstract, something foreign and removed from reality.

We must constantly note that attitudes arising from what intellectual life has become in the last centuries have created ethical and moral viewpoints. However, the question is, do these moral viewpoints have the power to affect outer reality? Do they have the power to be creative in outer reality?

Neither science nor moral points of view have been able to create a true bridge between what lives in people's spirit and what lies in material or natural processes. We see that over time the concerns of the human soul, the concerns of the human spirit, have become the intellectual monopoly, the cultural monopoly, of those groups who have made this or that credo their own. Thus, scientific endeavors have slowly become unaccustomed to concerning themselves with spirit and soul. People believe they are free from prejudice, that they follow a completely unprejudiced science, when they limit scientific methods to what is sense perceptible. People believe these methods immediately go beyond the bounds of human cognition when they enter the spiritual realm, when they enter the supersensible realm. People think that they are unprejudiced when, in fact, they are only following those forces that arise out of the historical course of events.

Those religious groups who, due to historical development, have had a monopoly in creating dogmas concerning the essence of spirit and soul out of old traditions, concerning the essence of human immortality, were in a position to prevent scientific research into these things. These groups applied pressure upon research until it simply succumbed to the pressure and accepted the dictates of the credo. Slowly the sciences came to believe they followed their own lack of prejudice, their own objectivity, because they were no longer conscious that what they actually followed are the prohibitions of the Church.

This "objective" approach has limited itself completely to external, sensible reality and has not endeavored to examine spiritual life with the conscientious methods that have brought modern science such great triumphs. It has, nonetheless, been able to affect the realm of spirit and soul. Thus the realm of spirit and soul has become something foreign to life. Life, external reality, is measured with exact methods. However, what concerns spirit and soul has slowly lost all living concepts. Those of you who follow the usual, the respected, the official textbooks and lectures on psychology and such will find in them nothing sparkling with life. Spiritual life has become something disconnected from life.

The only thing that could be a basis for the spiritual attitude of such people as Saint-Simon or Fourier or Louis Blanc when they considered social questions has remained unfruitful because nowhere were the living effects of the human spirit upon social reality taken into account. People go around talking in abstractions. With normal modern intellectuality, we cannot refute the statement that social facts can be observed only through economics, that no steps can be taken to fulfill human social longings. With only these means, we can make no counter argument when people insist that nothing results from spiritual life that could lead to a true healing of social relationships, that we must leave social development to the means of production. Modern intellectual life has become abstract. In a certain sense modern intellectual life is an ideology. Thus those who are, in the widest sense, members of socialist circles believe that *all* thinking must be ideological.

This is just what lies so heavily upon the souls of those who accept spiritual science. Spiritual science does not want to follow the same path taken by that burned-out academic science that has developed in modern times. Spiritual science wishes to lead people back to the true spirit. It wishes to lead people to an understanding of the true spiritual life to which they belong in just the same way that their bodies belong to physical reality, in the same way that through their material needs they are part of economic reality.

When we speak of real spirit today, when we attempt to speak of real spirit, we not only meet opposition, we meet mockery. We meet the kind of ridicule that derides all spiritual desires as pipe dreams or worse. We really meet modern disbelief when we say that what we mean as spirit cannot be comprehended with the usual powers of cognition that lead us through everyday life, through conventional science. We meet disbelief when we emphasize that to grasp and understand this spirit, it is necessary first to awaken powers of cognition that otherwise only sleep in human nature—in the same way that we awaken the usual powers of cognition in the developing child. Modern people will not admit that there could be something like an intellectual unpretentiousness, that there could be something like a further development of the inner human out of our childhood when we instinctively and dully step into life. They will not believe that we can awaken this later development to assist the normal powers of cognition, and that we can continue its development. But, it is not continued because modern intellectual life has resisted its continuance.

It is not our intent to speak in a vague way about spirit and its reality. Due to the spiritual development of the last centuries, it is easier to speak to the hearts and souls of people when we talk about spirit and spirituality in generalities instead of in a more definite manner. When people speak about spirit, they almost immediately think of spirit as an abstraction, something foreign to life. We might say that true spirit has become so foreign to them that they expect this spirit to reveal itself only in an occasional guest appearance.

Now I do not want to hold you up long with things common to the spiritualism to which modern thinking has fallen prey. In the end, however, what is this spiritualism other than the final decadent outstreaming of a desire for an abstract spiritual life! What we must understand is a true, concrete spiritual life to which human spirit can connect itself, and which we can grasp at every step in physical and cosmic reality. True spiritual life is not there to fulfill people's desires for theatrical effects, to show itself in spiritualist seances or in other ways desired by abstract mystics. The science of the spirit cannot speak of a spirit that partakes of guest appearances that have nothing to do with external reality, and are called forth simply to convince passive people that spirit exists. The science of the spirit cannot speak of such a spirit. Spiritual science can speak only of the spirit that in truth participates in every material effect and every material event. It speaks of the spirit with which people can connect themselves in order to master external reality. Thus, I will primarily speak about the activity of the spirit we must turn toward if we wish to learn how the spirit, working through people, can have an effect in life.

We first need to look at the way the spirit gradually develops out of the growing human. The growing child presents us with one of the greatest riddles of the world—a riddle we in education continuously try to solve. People have recently brought even this amazing riddle to a particularly abstract, nebulous height. Recently, there has been much talk about recognizing the power of education. People have recently made many attempts to use various educational principles. All such attempts have failed. They will stand as evidence of the goodwill of their proponents, but in the face of the great, the intense demands of our lives, these attempts must fail if they do not arise from a recognition of human essence.

People will not recognize human essence if they attempt to understand it only through modern science, or by intellectually assimilating the observations gained through science. Human essence reveals itself only if we understand how to observe it. It shows itself only if we develop the capability to investigate that certain something that reveals itself with every day, every week, every year after human beings enter into physical existence through birth or conception. We must observe the specific stages in the life of young humans if we do not want to remain in abstractions, but instead want to understand the spiritually concrete activity in external reality.

People value these things much too little today. For the observer of human essence, the stage when children change teeth, around six or seven years of age, indicates a deep change in the totality of human nature. If you have an organ that can truly examine such things empirically, the way we can empirically observe physical experiments in laboratories or in the astronomical observatory, then you can see such things. When you examine the life of the soul before this stage, you find that during the time preceding the change of teeth, people are primarily imitators. The imitative element, a kind of intuitive dependence upon the environment, motivates their entire being until seven years of age. In the first seven years of our lives we learn everything through imitation, through the most strict conformity to what is in our environment, right down to our movements, our gestures, our intonation.

In extreme cases, we can easily observe such things. I wish to mention only one of the many cases that become obvious if you have any sense at all for such things in life. I could mention a hundred others. I knew a young child who limped. Even though there was nothing wrong, the child limped, and people could not get her to stop limping. The reason the child limped was that she had an older sibling who, due to a diseased leg, actually had cause to limp! This imitative principle that motivates people until the change of teeth is thus expressed in an extreme case.

The true observer sees that quite new forces enter into the human life of body, soul and spirit when the change of teeth is complete. Then, what children perceive in their environment does not motivate them as much. Instead, they are especially ready to believe, to accept, what they feel to be the opinion or the belief of those who, through age or bearing, they intuitively perceive as authorities.

Until the time of puberty, this acceptance, this automatic acceptance of authority, is like a law of human nature. If you wish to properly affect the human essence during this time, then you must turn to this intuitive principle of authority.

Those who, without prejudice, without some pet theory, observe the life of young people, those who work with facts, know how much it can mean for their whole life if children have someone they can look up to as an authority. You need only observe how people's feelings about such an authority change! You need only observe what later in life results from these feelings toward authority! Everything that we develop as truly free independent democratic feelings in human social life, everything that we gain in true human understanding and human respect, is at heart a result of appropriate development under intuitive authority during the period from the change of teeth until puberty.

We should not meddle with such things through special programs. We should approach this area through purely empirical observation. Then we will discover what we need to think and feel when we receive the school child who has developed in imitation of the care—or the neglect—of the parents. We will see how we must work out of the principle of authority in school if we truly want to work appropriately. We can only be effective when we derive our pedagogical methods and develop our whole teaching activity out of a human understanding.

If you are not able to observe from year to year, from week to week how other demands develop out of the core of the child and rise to the surface, then you will not be able to work *with* human developmental powers, you will work *against* them. Educational material and methods must, in fact, meet these requirements of the developing child.

If you do not know how authority works, if you do not know the intimate interactions that exist between the authority and the growing child, then you will never be able to work positively in the education of children this age. I wish to mention a single concrete example. You know that due to certain programs and prejudices, there is now much discussion concerning visual aids.[1] You are supposed to show the children everything. This often implies that you should teach the children only about things you can place before their eyes, or at least demonstrate to their intellect, so that they can immediately understand everything with their immature comprehension.

You need only look at the books that are to serve as guides for such teaching. Certainly, illustrative material is, within bounds, quite appropriate. But, what is appropriate within certain boundaries leads to error when we extend it beyond these boundaries. Visual aids—as I mentioned, you can see it in the guides—often lead to extremely materialistic triviality. People try to limit instruction to what children can understand, to what such people, in their simplemindedness, believe is the maximum children can understand. However, they neglect something. They do not take into account what teaching out of authority means to human life. Individuals who are thirty-five years old may, due to some event, suddenly remember that when they were seven, eight, nine or ten years old, they learned something in school from a highly regarded authority. They say

---

1. See note, p. 87.

to themselves, "I did not really understand it then. I only looked with high regard to that honored authority. When that honored authority said something, led something into my soul, I knew it instinctively. I did not know how I knew it, but I felt it was something valuable. I remembered it, perhaps only as words, but it lived in me for many years afterward. After many years, now that I have become mature, I recall what I learned long ago." When people are mature, these recollections of things they accepted in youth upon simple authority now become a source of strength. They now know what it means that things they learned as children can first be fully understood as recollections in later life. In this way, we can give people living strength!

I wish to mention one other thing about the intimate workings between educational authority and the child. We want to teach the child certain things meant for a later period in life. Of course, the child does not understand these things. Thus, we clothe them in all kinds of allegories and pictures. Let us take a picture someone might think of, for instance, the picture of immortality. The teacher might say, "Here you have the cocoon of a butterfly. The animal is nestled within it. It will creep out, the beautiful butterfly will come out of the cocoon." Now, the teacher might go further and say, "Just as the butterfly is in this cocoon, in the same way the immortal soul lies within your body. When you go through the gates of death, this immortal soul will appear in the spiritual world just as the butterfly will appear here. Remember how here in the physical world the beautiful butterfly comes out of the cocoon."

You can make such a picture. It may touch the child. But, such a picture will not achieve what it should achieve if, as a teacher, you only have the consciousness that you are clever and the child is dumb, and that, therefore, you have to clothe in a picture what the child cannot yet understand. There are great intangibles in living human relationships. Regardless of what occurs between the intellect of the authority and the child's intellect, something will happen in the child's subconscious that comes from the discrepancy between the teacher's disbelief in the picture and the intent to develop the child's belief through the picture.

You need only observe how differently things occur—this is something paradoxical—when you yourself believe that the picture of the cocoon and the butterfly is not simply a picture, when you are clear that *you* do not make this picture, but the creative natural powers themselves make this picture. The one and only great artist, Natura, forms this picture. She carries her divinity within her in such a way that this picture expresses the same thing at a lower level as immortality expresses at a higher level. In other words, when you have complete belief in the picture, when it is not something made up for someone else, when it is your own inner belief, then something occurs in your telling of it to the child. Then, when it affects the child in the proper way, later in life the grown child's soul will carry a true picture of immortality. Today we must not judge the things connected with the principle of authority by appearances. To really understand what occurs in people's lives, we need, at the least, a careful study from the standpoint I will discuss in a moment. We need such a study to understand what to use in education during the period between the change of teeth and puberty.

Real capabilities of judgment, of free, independent reason, first appear in human nature after puberty. If we activate this independent reason too early, if we appeal too much to the child's intellect before puberty, then we do not appeal to what can be given from one person to another through authority. Then we kill much of what we need to develop between the ages of six to seven and fourteen to fifteen, that is, during the time of elementary school.

Now we must ask, where will the teachers gain insight into the forces they must use, first when the child is an imitator, then when the child is between the change of teeth and puberty, and then in that stage of life after puberty? Our detractors can mock, they can ridicule what spiritual science means when it says that particular powers, higher powers of cognition, must be formed in human nature so that people can recognize the spiritual and its actions in the different ages of human life.

In my book *How to Know Higher Worlds,* I have described in detail how people can obtain these higher powers of cognition. The same thing is in the second part of my *Outline of Occult Science,* and in other books. I have shown how people can use common everyday cognition, common scientific cognition, as a basis to rise through three higher stages that I have called (do not be disturbed by the names, you have to use some common names) Imaginative cognition, Inspired cognition and Intuitive cognition.

We can obtain Imaginative cognition when we systematically do quite specific meditations that I describe in the above-named books, when we train thinking beyond the level of normal life and conventional science. Imaginative cognition first gives us the possibility of developing pictures in our soul life, pictures that are not spatial, not fantasy, but that represent spiritual reality.

People learn to recognize that, in the end, everything humans develop as ideas, as conceptions, as sense perceptions for normal life and for conventional science is connected to human physical existence. We learn to slowly disengage the life of the soul from simple bodily life as we increasingly undertake to raise our powers of thinking to a meditative activity. We rise to an Imaginative cognition that at first consists only of pictures, but that shows us reality the moment we further develop ourselves as I describe in the above-mentioned books. When the Inspiration (which we have first prepared ourselves to be capable of comprehending) enters from the spiritual world that is just as much around us as the physical world, then the effects of the spiritual world fill these pictures.

If we then rise to Intuitive cognition, we will meet spiritual beings in just the same way we meet physical beings in the physical world. Today I can merely mention this and must direct you to the books where I describe these things in detail. If we can really rise to what I call Imaginative, Inspired and Intuitive cognition, then these stages of cognition are not phantasms, are not daydreams as our contemporaries, with their lack of spirituality, call them. When they are feeling kindly, they say at best, "Well, all right, the product of a sick mind!" However, they will judge differently if we only indicate the true basis, the real source of this higher knowledge—and I will do that today by referring to a characteristic I have mentioned before. Where in human nature do these forces lie that we must develop in life so that we can look into the spiritual world?

Think for a moment. We have certain forces that make us into imitative beings until the change of teeth, forces that, in a certain sense, later recede. These forces find no further use in normal modern social life—they recede. However, they remain connected with human nature. Again, there are the forces that act between the change of teeth and puberty to stimulate the inclination toward authority out of the soul-physical realm. These forces, which I described in connection with the intangibles living between the teacher and the children, are real forces in childhood, but they, too, later recede.

Furthermore, as human beings we have forces that are active from puberty until around the age of twenty that also later recede. (Of course, now we seldom see what we call youthful idealism, youthful motivations that lead to living ideals. At one time people perceived living ideals in the same way that we perceive external life.) These are the same forces that after puberty first form the foundation of true judgment and that need to be brought to a special level of development. They also recede after the age of twenty-one or twenty-two.

In the last centuries, human life has developed such that we only cultivate intellectual capabilities, scientific capabilities, the ability to observe natural and social things. To the extent that this development has taken place, those powers active in the first three stages of life have receded. We can, however, bring them forth again. Imaginative cognition is nothing more than those forces whose spiritual activity forms the human body and soul from puberty until the age of twenty. It is nothing more than those soul forces that, under the direction of my book *How To Know Higher Worlds,* we can bring forth out of the depths of human nature. The spiritual researcher brings forth again what has receded. Where it otherwise remains hidden, we bring it forth again so that it enters into consciousness. Then it develops Imaginative cognition.

It is more difficult to bring forth those human forces that are active from the change of teeth until puberty but that recede later in life and lie deep in the organism. However, through such exercises as I have described in my books, we can call them, too, into consciousness. These prove to be identical with forces that are active in children, but remain unknown and unnoticed by science. We learn how to master these forces. Through an Inspired cognition, they bring into our consciousness certain spiritual secrets of our surroundings. This is not a made-up force, not something that does not already exist in life. This is something that proves itself to be active during the most important developmental years. Spiritual research brings it forth again to become the basis of insight into the spiritual world.

Because they remain hidden from observation, the most difficult forces to bring forth are those forces that are active in human nature between birth, we can even say between conception, and the change of teeth. Those forces find their conclusion in the permanent teeth and later completely withdraw into the human organic system. Nevertheless, we can bring these forces forth after we have called forth the others.

We see that we now connect ourselves with these forces when we grasp them with our full being, these forces that actually gave us the life impulse. In a certain sense, we unroll in the first seven years of our life—we bring forth out of our deepest souls the actual impulse, which we recognize as spirit, that we received in the first stage of life. When we bring into our consciousness what has receded, then we have Intuitive cognition. We do not connect ourselves only with our own being, but with something in comparison to which our normal thoughts are absurdities. We connect ourselves with something that is one and the same as the Being of the World. We then recognize the spirit in us as connected to the Spirit of the World.

You see, teachers who understand human beings through spiritual science, who have the developing human before them, look at what the spirit forms out of this developing human. The teachers meet this developing human with their educational skills. The teacher working from spiritual science does not have in mind a pedagogy used to educate children according to abstract rules, as is normal today. For this teacher, each child is a riddle. What should come to life in each child is something the teacher must solve in a living way every day, in every hour. However, when the teacher acquires the viewpoint of this living, working spirit in the living development of the child, he or she absorbs a recognition of reality that does not remain in concepts, does not remain in abstract generalities, but permeates the will with spirit. Such a teacher really becomes a pillar of knowledge, and he or she will develop a truly living pedagogy because it comes from an understanding of the human being, from a recognition of the complete, whole person.

Spiritual science is nothing other than what we can create out of the forces that are spiritually active in the stages of human development. It is not some fantasy. The source for the development of higher spiritual powers does not come from just anything that might arise in people, but from the conscious apprehension of what works in the healthiest forces of growth and life in the first three stages of human development. In that we become spiritual researchers, we raise into the consciousness of our understanding of the world and of people what really causes our growth and development as human beings.

So closely related is Anthroposophy to the spiritual sword and shield of cognition! For that reason, spiritual science is not something we can take up simply through our intellect. Since we bring it forth out of the being and growth forces of the whole human, it permeates our whole being, our feeling and will. It becomes a basic human force. Immaturity and unconsciousness are concepts that lose their relevance through the activity of the spirit in human beings. We may not say that people lose their instinctive, basic forces when they consciously develop the spirit. No, this remains. The same basic strength that is otherwise present only in instinctive actions is present when the spirit permeates people in this way. The spirit really enters into the being of the teacher, into the effectiveness of the teacher, into those who are to develop social pedagogical forces in youth. What spiritual science is comes from the same source from which people themselves grow. Self-development is only a transformation of our growth forces.

You see, these are things, at least in their underlying principles, that modern people often regard much as people once viewed the science of Copernicus and Galileo. What most people once viewed as an absurdity has now become a matter of course. In the same way, the knowledge of the three stages of life, their basic forces and their transformation into Imagination, Inspiration and Intuition through spiritual science will become a matter of course.

Our age can notice that modern intellectual life (I have shown this in two examples) has become powerless in the face of social life and social desires. When modern people see that the intellectualism developed in the last centuries (abstract, foreign and removed from life) is not the only possibility, that there is also a science that comes from the transformation of growth forces, they will develop sympathy and interest. This spiritual science can understand the living spirit that does not play guest roles in life, but is present and active in life; and the human spirit, by connecting itself with that living spirit, develops social pedagogical strength.

Why (again we put this question) are we so seldom able to transform into social will what we receive in ideas, what we develop in ideas? How is it that such disbelief has arisen that people speak only of ideology when they refer to the power of the spirit?

The period that is just behind us was a time of great triumphs for modern science. Those great scientific triumphs could arise only when people first turned away from what was within them and devoted themselves to the activities of nature and to the scientific method. Those who are spiritual researchers will certainly recognize the conscientiousness, the exactitude, of modern scientific methods, and will also recognize the fertility of these methods within their areas. They will certainly not go into a simplistic, unsympathetic criticism of limited and bounded material knowledge. However, we must be clear about one fact of experience that people do not observe today. People do not observe it because they can see, completely correctly from at least one point of view, that scientific methods are well suited to give a picture of natural phenomena. Because scientific methods work so well in this realm, people are not inclined to ask how this experience, derived in this way, affects the whole essence of humanity.

Concerning observations of nature and the recognition of natural laws, people accept only what their senses believe and their intellect can process. They consciously shut out everything that comes from their feeling and will life. What they understand about nature does not affect the will and feeling life. Thus, many people who view the entire situation without prejudice speak about modern science and its effects differently than those who simply accept all the great scientific triumphs.

If we look at the human essence, the picture we can achieve through the scientific method has something fatalistic about it—it is something that fills only our intellect, but does not touch our will. If we use the scientific method in popular or scientific thinking about social life, then social life in a sense ebbs away, falls apart. Just as something finely ground runs through a sieve, true social life slips past our observation when we approach it only with modern scientific methods. We can see how strict causal scientific thinking fails the moment it is applied to the social realm or general external society. I want to give an example of this: There is perhaps no other book in a much-debated area that so beautifully develops exact scientific thinking as *Das Werden der Organismen, eine Widerlegung der Darwinschen Zufallstheorie* (The development of the organism—a rebuttal of the Darwinian theory of chance), by the well-known biologist, Oskar Hertwig. We can offer only the highest praise for this book's attempt to characterize conventional scientific insights into the theory of evolution.

A short time after Hertwig's book appeared, he also published something about social, legal and political issues, issues concerning general society. It would be impossible to think of something more dilettantish and incompetent than this first-rate biologist's stroll through an area generally encompassed by the concept "social life"!

There are hundreds, thousands, of such examples. They all show what we can directly observe, namely, that even the highest devotion to natural scientific knowledge causes us to fill our consciousness with ideas that are actually the content of an ideology that cannot pulse into our feeling and will. These ideas remain unfruitful in feeling and willing.

I want to expressly emphasize that in considering such things, it is not my intention to go in the reverse direction. I do not wish to contend that the way of thinking of the vast majority of modern people is simply the outcome of the scientific way of thinking. No, quite the opposite. The last centuries have brought forth a certain kind of common thinking. Those who really study history, not simply a *fable convenue,* a convenient story, see how human life, particularly social life right down to the peasantry, has changed in the last three or four centuries. What has come forth as natural scientific thinking is, in my opinion, only an external expression of what has generally taken hold of human soul life. I do not wish to call human thinking and feeling a product of modern scientific attitude and knowledge, but just the opposite. I see in the scientific attitude and knowledge only the external symbol, the revelation, of what is the *general* direction of human thinking, the general attitude toward life and external reality.

What has developed is the basis for a thinking and feeling foreign to life, for a spiritual life foreign to life. If, on the other hand, you consider what forms the basis of spiritual science (I have just shown that this spiritual science is only a transformation of the human forces of growth and development), then you can rise to see a real world in these things. Then what we take in with spiritual knowledge enters into our powers of feeling and will. This is the only healthy way for people now and in the near future to come to a truly social willing. It is necessary for the future to infuse this social willing with the knowledge that can come from the spiritual.

We would not say that everyone can effortlessly achieve the development of higher spiritual powers. We certainly do not at all contend that. Certainly, only a few people will be able to recognize the secrets of spiritual life through direct vision of the highest spiritual facts. This recognition is first connected to a certain inner courage, a certain boldness. Human will, human intellectual power, all human soul forces must develop so that they extend beyond the normal level of strength. These soul forces must grow so they can grasp the spiritual world that flits past ordinary human cognition, the spiritual world people cannot usually perceive. In a certain sense, we must reach for the finest among everyday capacities. The spirit does not come in the same way that external realities come. The spirit comes when you connect yourself with it in the same way that you feel pain, that you feel desire and distress that flood through your soul, as something very real. In this way you will feel, experience and recognize the spiritual through a flooding in your soul, only you know that it is not something simply subjective like desire and distress. It is so intimately connected with the soul, like desire and distress, joy and sorrow, yet it streams into our souls as something foreign, something spiritual. At first, it will be something unexpected. We expect something quite different in external life. Thus, we must accept this spiritual life in sorrow and pain, since we receive and perceive around us a life that we do not expect. No one comes into the spiritual world who does not struggle for this entrance, step by step, through sorrow and pain. This, though, only concerns *research* of the spiritual world.

In contrast, we must say that the capacities to *understand* what spiritual research has to say comprise only ordinary healthy common sense. For spiritual researchers, it is unimportant simply to assure others that they love truth and see what they speak of as spiritual. Rather, spiritual researchers can speak so that people with healthy common sense can understand their path of thinking. Of course, their thinking is formed from spiritual vision. However, people can recognize that it has the same inner logic they learn from external, sense-perceptible reality. Thus, if it is not limited by opposing prejudices, healthy common sense can judge whether spiritual researchers talk nonsense. Healthy common sense can judge from the way spiritual researchers speak whether the spiritual world is open to them, whether they really see into it. Thus, what individual spiritual researchers bring into social life is itself a social pedagogical force.

If people accustom themselves to acquiring understanding, to acquiring the healthy common sense to be able to perceive the convincing power of what spiritual science reveals as the true reality of human life, then they will develop another social force. This social force will lead people to one another and will bring into the structure of the social organism things that cannot come into it any other way. These things form a more intimate recognition of one person by another, an ability to accept other people, a germination of true social impulses.

This is what develops in human interactions based upon true spiritual cognition and everything connected with it. People will feel how social pedagogical forces can enter social will when they begin to extend what we can draw from human growth and development into the living social organism. Only then will they understand that human essence embodies social organs. People will be able to bring into the social organism what they understand of the spirit working in the natural organism.

People will not come to true social pedagogical strength until they are able to draw social pedagogical forces from the motives, from the impulses, of spiritual knowledge!

Where does our understanding of spiritual scientific knowledge come from? It comes from those diminished forces that made physical and spiritual adults from little children. We do not need to let those forces lie fallow, we need to use them. We need only to apply our own humanity to external social order for a true social pedagogical strength to develop in the education of children. Then, too, that indefinable but very real activity in education that lies in human relationships, in human interactions, will develop between us. If we will only understand what meets us from the personality of the whole person, if we will only understand what mysterious things lie in each person, how individuals can, in their sub- and super-consciousness, grow beyond themselves, then a social pedagogical strength will exist in human interactions. We will so interact with one another that the being of one raises and carries the being of the other. In short, social pedagogical strength flows out of spiritual recognition, not only for the education of children, but for the totality of human life.

You see, the idea of the threefold social organism does not, in truth, come from some program, like so many social ideas. It comes from a new spiritual direction for which, on the one side, modern people have only very little sympathy. But, on the other side, they yearn for it with all of their subconscious desires and instincts. They thirst for it. Much more than people consciously believe, they carry in their subconscious a thirst for the spiritual. Today we see that people clothe their social desires in all sorts of formulas, forms and demands. What is characteristic about them, if you look at what meets us from people's well-meaning will forces, from correct rightful needs, is that they cannot generally be understood. They cannot be so understood that genuinely constructive activity could arise from them.

This is quite characteristic, and it is very remarkable the way those people who have worked for years on ideas and programs for social reform, the way all their thinking, everything they have derived from their spiritual life, fails. Recently a letter from a well-known social revolutionary appeared in the newspapers, a letter from Kropotkin to George Brandes. In it Kropotkin describes the bleak situation in eastern Europe. In his way, he really describes the whole European situation, and concludes, "Yes, the only thing we can hope for is that we are given bread and tools to produce bread."

You see a social revolutionary, who has for years attempted to think about his ideas, has come so far as to state that the world is to be organized so that the tools to produce bread shall be properly provided, so that people can be fed. In the end, only an abstract cry for bread and tools results! Disbelief in abstract spirituality, in his own spirituality!

We have to see through the cry for bread, to see that it is nothing other than a modern cry for the spirit. Only out of an understanding of the *true* spirit can come the social strength of will that can properly provide tools for bread production. The point is not to cry for programs, but to turn rightly to human faculties, to turn to the strength of human activity. That means to correctly understand people, so that they find their proper place in life and can work in the most efficient way to feed their families, to work for the whole life of their fellow human beings.

We must make the social question a question of humanity in the broadest sense. Otherwise, no good will come of it. It is possible to improve things when we recognize that the social question is complete only when we perceive it out of the spirit.

What we strive for in the threefolding of the social organism arises out of a new spiritual direction, out of a recognition of the demands that are so nebulous today. Although they are correct, they are nonetheless nebulous. What we strive for arises out of the recognition that an unconscious longing for this new spirituality lives in these demands. Everything we recognize as decadence in the striving for spirituality is an expression of people's still clumsy search for the spirit. Certainly, one of the most decadent forms of this search is spiritism, or false mystical paths. This decadent direction has come out of centuries, we can even say in this case millennia, of education through which people have not learned to search for the spirit in reality itself, in the reality to which they belong. The striving toward spirituality has been carried to such abstract heights because dogmatic monopolies wanted to usurp it.

Spiritual science wants to prove that the same powers that can grasp external nature, if we develop them further as I described today, can also penetrate spiritual life. Then people will not strive toward an abstract spirit, toward a spirit created for the occasional gratification of human consciousness, but toward a spirit that is in reality, that is *one* with material life. We do not recognize the spirit when we look at matter simply as matter, and say that it is only matter and the spirit is somewhere else. No. Those who seek the spirit through abstract formulations and think they should seek it along the path of spiritism, for instance, in the dark corners of life, have not yet achieved the correct human relationship to the spirit.

We have achieved the proper human relationship to spiritual life only if we seek such a spirit as we can see in nature around us, particularly in human life itself, in the life of children, in social connections. We have achieved the correct relationship when we know that in everything around us, even in economic life, the spirit is active, and when we search in such a way that we connect this spiritual activity to ourselves. A proper seeking of the spirit exists only when people want to understand the spirit, only when they love the spirit that is active in themselves. It exists only when people can form a bridge between the spiritual reality in themselves and the spiritual reality in the world. Only through such a spirit and through the knowledge of such a spirit can we develop the social pedagogical strength that we need for human life now and in the near future.

Thus, we can only repeat time and again:

May the dark unconscious desires living in human hearts and minds flame up into the conscious life of soul, so that humanity may find, in this age when social concern has become so bright, the *true* spiritual power of the world with which inner spiritual powers of humans can connect.

Out of this union between the World Spirit and the human spirit will flow the best source of social pedagogical strength for human life.

After a short discussion, Dr. Steiner concluded with the following:

Now, of course, those who speak out of spiritual science will not be of the opinion that what has come forth recently as science, philosophy or art needs to be thrown away simply because it has led to the false path mentioned by the previous speaker. However, the essence of spiritual science should be that the one-sided human activities that arose in the last centuries out of modern scientific assumptions should give up their one-sidedness and merge into a general stream of all-encompassing life.

You will not expect that I am in any way against what science, philosophy or the arts have generated within their rightful boundaries, if you follow not only my spiritual scientific books but also, for example, my description of the progress of philosophy in *The Riddles of Philosophy*. If you look at the way I have interpreted the essence of art—the Goetheanum in Dornach that houses the School for Spiritual Science, which, in its external appearance, attempts to represent spiritual science—you will not see an opposition to the modern developments in science, philosophy or art, to the extent that they occur within their proper limits. The one-sidedness that has come forth in these areas seems to me even to be something necessary. Life develops in contradictions, even polar contradictions. Thus, if we introspectively consider history, we can see that periods when certain activities were one-sided alternate with periods when these activities flow into a certain universal, consonant, harmonious life activity. However, it is the fructification of modern scientific views, of philosophical considerations and modern artistic trends that spiritual science should particularly accentuate.

Let us take, for example, to use something that I could barely mention in the lecture, many of the more modern trends in art. Certainly, we can easily make fun of such trends in art. But, you see, even though certain things like expressionist art appear incomplete to our souls, nevertheless we must say that they are only a preliminary, often clumsy attempt to come to something that is really in accordance with life. In the last century, we have slipped into a kind of intellectuality. Intellectuality is unfruitful. In social life and in art, what has been the consequence? The necessary consequence has been that although people have wanted to be artistically active, they have slipped into naturalism, into the simple imitation of nature.

The simple imitation of nature can never be art in an absolute sense. I say that not in deference to the art critics, but simply because when someone so strongly imitates what they see in external nature, they will never reach nature. If you have a sense for it, you will always prefer nature over what simply imitates nature.

An outrageously inept thing often occurs (you will excuse me if I bring up this trivial example) that is the expression of outrageously bad taste. You show people, let's say, an apple that you find particularly pleasing, beautifully polished, and so forth. Then, you say, "It's as though it were made out of wax!" It is impossible to think of something more outrageously inept than when someone compares something from nature with an artificial thing, regardless of how good this artificial thing is! For the simple reason that we can never reach true nature in art, we must reject absolute naturalism.

It is something quite different if, in the expressionist manner, the artist wants to embody something that people experience beyond what is simply natural—even though the embodiment may be clumsy. However, to recognize that clumsy beginnings should be neither over- nor undervalued, you must be open to what is today often expressed by a slogan, but which, in connection with human life, people do not correctly understand.

The following may sound like a paradox. I certainly belong among those who have the highest admiration for Raphael. However, from my point of view the only people who have a right to admire Raphael are those who are convinced that if someone today were to paint just as Raphael painted, it would be impossible and inconsistent with modern times. It would not be art that we could accept today as contemporary art. This may sound paradoxical. However, what has occurred during human development belongs to its particular stage. You must really take this whole idea of development seriously. What developed since the middle of the fifteenth century in science, philosophy and art is completely justifiable as an educational impulse in developing humanity. However, human development has today reached a stage where it must strive for the other pole. As humans, we needed to go through a one-sided science for a time. We needed to absorb the thoughts of this science, to come to a mood of soul brought about by our noticing the powerlessness of these scientific thoughts. This powerlessness calls forth a counterforce in the active soul life, the counterforce toward spiritual recognition, toward a spiritual viewpoint.

If you take Lessing's thoughts earnestly, that history is an education of humanity, then you can best come to grips with such things. Thus, today in certain areas people's prejudices allow what spiritual science has to offer to enter directly into social pedagogy, that is, into external reality.

It has been possible to make artistically visible in the Dornach building what moves us inwardly, to express in forms what moves us inwardly. I might also mention that only very recently has it been possible to attempt to found a school upon real pedagogy. Our friend Emil Molt integrated the founding of the Waldorf School in Stuttgart into a modern industrial undertaking (people are beside themselves in ridicule over this), into the Waldorf cigarette factory in Stuttgart. Here we can now build a unified elementary school upon what can result for pedagogy from an understanding of the spiritual point of view. I held the pedagogical seminar for the faculty of the Waldorf School, and I must say that this belongs among the most beautiful of things I could imagine as a task for myself. There, a pedagogy was founded that does not exist to fulfill norms imagined as necessary to train people, but rather a pedagogy that results from a true understanding of the whole person, that is, the body, soul and spirit of human beings. This is a pedagogy that paradoxically makes life more difficult for the teacher than it would be with simple, normative education.

Those who believe in standardized education, who preach programs, who give educational principles, know how to instruct. However, those who teach directly from life can only receive impulses to observe what really occurs in the developing human being, from year to year, from week to week, from month to month. Even though it may be a large class, you must continuously be in living interactions. You must understand what it means not to practice a learned pedagogy from memory, but to invent at each moment the individual methods that this child needs.

What is effective in life cannot be based in memory or in habit. What we have in our memory, what we practice from memory in our human activities, what we practice out of habit is something that in all cases is simply a cliché. What results from spiritual life can never be a cliché!

There have been times, and probably still will be, when I have lectured on the same theme week after week. I do not think anyone can say I have ever spoken about the same theme in exactly the same way. When you speak from the spirit, your concern is to create something immediate. It is not at all possible in the normal sense to memorize what comes from the spirit, because it must continuously develop in direct contact with life. For those who are active out of the spirit, the simple memorization of spiritual knowledge is about the same as if someone were to say, "I am not going to eat today because I ate yesterday; why should I eat again today? My body will continue simply on the basis of what I ate yesterday." Yes, our physical organism is such that it continuously renews itself. This is also true for the spirit. The spirit must also be within this vigorous life. The true spirit must at all times be a creator. In the same way, education carried by the spirit must be a continuously creative art.

There will be no blessing upon our elementary schools, and there will also be no healing in our school systems, until education becomes a continuously living, creating art, carried by true love and those intangibles of which I have spoken.

We can see in all areas how necessary it is in the face of the unconscious and subconscious demands of modern humanity (and in the near future it will be even more necessary) to take what people wish to make into a comfortable intellectual program and go from that to a truly productive experience of the spirit. This will be much less comfortably achieved than a great deal of what people today call spiritual life. However, this will become the social pedagogical force that we need. On the one hand, it is true that after so many years of devotion to scientific thinking the innermost souls of modern people long for a direct recognition of the spirit. It is on the other hand true that social demands cry for a spiritual deepening. It is true that the subject of my lecture is not something thought of haphazardly, but something heard from contemporary human development. However, you must first educate yourselves to it and connect yourselves with it.

In conclusion, I would like to point out one other thing that is particularly necessary now. Because everyone thinks that some fruitful philosophical life can result from subjective opinions, we must indicate how to understand questions today. I want to do that with an example.

Many years ago I held a lecture in a southern German city in which I spoke about the Christian saints. There were two priests at the lecture. Since they could say nothing against the content of the lecture, they came to me and said, "We don't have anything to say against the content of what you said today. However, we do want to say something about the fact that you claim to speak for people whose path leads them to your way of thinking. We, however, speak for all people." This is what they said. I, of course, addressed them with their proper title. You must always be polite. I said, "You see, Reverend, you believe that you speak for all people. I find that natural and reasonable since, subjectively, that is the case. However, whether I speak, or whether you believe that you speak, for all people doesn't mean anything, particularly not in the present when individual human lives exist so much in the whole of society. Today we must learn not to define our tasks by subjective arbitrariness, but to develop them individually out of objectivity and objective facts. And so I ask you, Reverend, if you think that you speak for all people, then look at the facts. Does everyone go to church?" There they could not say yes! You see, thus speak the facts. I then said to them, "I speak for those who no longer come to you in the church." That is what the facts teach us today.

Things do not merely guide us in the direction of an objection. Rather, we must see the facts as they are and let them form the argument. It is something quite natural that people think that they speak for everyone.

What is important today is that (although we can know that the majority of people consciously resist real spiritual scientific impulses) if we can understand the revelation, we can also know that these impulses have the effect of a subconscious cry, "Make whole again what has split into philosophy, science, art, religion and the other areas, especially the social areas, of culture!"

However, we can only make these things whole according to their own spirit. Only then do things speak to us not out of the abstract, but out of a concrete unity where the true spirit that we find in all individual things is the one spirit in everything.

However, because the unifying spirit is something concretely alive, we cannot understand it by encompassing it with abstract concepts, with ideology. We must resolve to seek the living spirit. We can only seek it, though, if, with a certain intellectual modesty, we find the bridge between the sleeping inner human forces that are of a spiritual nature and the spirit that lives in nature, in human life, in the whole cosmos. Thus, in concluding, I wish to emphasize once again that we must take into account the longing that lives in the depths of the human soul to bind the human spirit with the Spirit of the World. Much of the solution to humanity's burning questions lies in this bond between human spirit and World Spirit.

I do not want to arouse the belief that we can solve every problem. However, humanity is on the path to a partial resolution of riddles that have always been presented to it. In this partial resolution lies true human progress in that we recognize how the spirit lives in everything, and how this spirit can light the way if we awaken the spirit in ourselves. The greatest, most important contemporary social tasks live in this recognition, and it will lead to healing when wider and wider circles realize this.

6

Spiritual Science and Pedagogy

BASEL—NOVEMBER 27, 1919

A Lecture for Public School Teachers

I consider it a particular honor to be able to speak to you about the relationship of my work in spiritual science to your pedagogical work. You will allow me to make two introductory remarks. The first is that I will, of course, need to clothe my thoughts in apparently theoretical words and ideas, since to discuss points of view, we need words. However, I expressly note that I do not speak theoretically. I would not even speak about today's topic if I did not direct a portion of my activity toward the practical, particularly concerning educational methods and their effectiveness. Thus, what I wish to bring to you today comes directly from practice.

The second thing I would like to say is that at present spiritual science is extremely controversial. I therefore can quite understand (especially because I represent spiritual science) that there may be many objections today because its methods are, in many cases, foreign to modern points of view. Perhaps we can help make spiritual science more understandable through the way we introduce it and attempt to make it a true living force in such an important practical area as education.

Can we name any areas of life that are unaffected by pedagogical activities and interests? At an age when children can develop themselves into everything possible, we entrust them to those who act as teachers. Teachers can provide what humanity needs only through the warmest participation in the totality of human life. When I speak about the special topic of spiritual science and pedagogy, I do this because, particularly now, the science of the spirit should become an active part of life. Spiritual science should be present to reunite the separate human cultural interests that have been driven apart in the last centuries, particularly in the nineteenth century. Through spiritual science, through a concrete point of view, we can unite the specialties without becoming paralyzed by the requirements of specialization. Today, there is also a very important reason to think about the relationship of spiritual science to pedagogy: education has influenced all human thinking and activity, including modern science and its great achievements.

More than people know, the scientific way of thinking that has led to such glorious results in science has won influence over everything we do, particularly over what we do in education. Although I am unable to develop the foundations of spiritual science here, I wish to take note of one thing, namely, the relationship of the scientific method to life.

Think, for example, about the human eye, this marvel through which we experience the outside world in a particular realm of the senses. The eye, this marvelous organ, is constructed so as to see the world and at the same time (I speak comparatively) always to forget itself in this seeing. In a sense, when we really want to investigate this instrument of external vision, we must completely reverse the standpoint of observation that modern science can only approximate. While seeing, we cannot at the same time look back at the essence of our eyes. We can use this picture to relate the scientific method to life. In modern times we have carefully and conscientiously developed the scientific method so that it gives the different sciences an objective picture of the external world. In doing this, we have formed a basic mood of soul such that we forget the human self in the scientific observation of the world, such that we forget everything directly connected with human life. Thus, it has come about that the more we develop in a modern scientific sense, the less we can use this science to see what is human.

The desire of spiritual science to bring about that reversal of observation that again turns to human beings arises from an understanding of science that goes beyond the understanding conventional science has of itself. This reversal can only occur when people go through those stages of soul life that I have described in *How To Know Higher Worlds,* and in an abbreviated form have indicated in the second part of *An Outline of Occult Science.* These are the processes that really carry this life of the human soul beyond normal life, and beyond the normal scientific world.

To come to such a manner of looking at things, you must have what I would like to call intellectual modesty. In a recent public lecture here, I gave a picture of what is necessary. Suppose, for example, we observe a five-year-old child. Suppose we put a book of Goethe's lyrical poetry in the hands of a five-year-old child. This book of Goethe's poems contains a whole world. The child will take the book in hand and play around with it, but will not perceive anything that actually speaks to people from this volume. However, we can develop the child, that is, we can develop the soul powers sleeping in the child, so that in ten or twelve years the child can really take from the volume what it contains. We need this attitude if we are to find our way to the science of the spirit. We must be able to say to ourselves that even the most careful education of our intellect, of our methods of observation and experimentation, brings us only so far. From there on, we can take over our own development. From that stage on, we can develop the previously sleeping forces ourselves. Then we will become aware that previously we stood in the same relationship to the external nature of our spirit-soul being, particularly the essence of our humanity, as the five-year-old child to the volume of Goethe's lyrical poetry. In essence and in principle, everything depends upon a decision for intellectual modesty, so that we can find our way to the science of the spirit.

We achieve the capacity to really observe ourselves, to observe the human being, when we practice specific thinking, feeling and willing exercises developed to make thinking independent, to train the will, when we become increasingly independent from physical willing and thinking. If we can observe the human being, then we can also observe what is so extremely important, the developing human. Today, there is certainly much talk about the spirit, talk about independent thinking. The science of the spirit cannot agree with this talk for a simple reason. Spiritual science develops inner spiritual techniques to grasp and understand concrete spirituality, not the spirit about which people speak nebulously as forming the basis of things and people. Spiritual science must go into detail concerning the essence of the human being.

Today, we want to speak about the essence of the developing human. I would say that people speak quite abstractly about human individuality and its development. However, they are quite correctly conscious that the teacher especially needs to take the development of this human individuality into account. I only wish to point out that insightful teachers are very clear about how little our modern science of education is able to identify the orderly stages of human development. I would like to give two examples. The oft-mentioned Viennese educator Theodor Vogt represented the reformed Herbartian school of thought. He said that we are not advanced enough in our understanding of human history to derive a view of child development from human historical development in the same way biologists derive the individual human embryonic development from the development of the species. The pedagogue Rein repeated this point of view. It culminates in accepting that today we do not have research methods of any sort that could identify the basis of human development. The development of such capacities as those I have just cursorily mentioned (you can read more in my books) enables us to approach the riddle that meets us so wonderfully when we observe how, from birth onward, an inner human force increasingly appears in every gesture. In particular, we can see how it manifests through speech, through the relationships of people with their surroundings, and so forth. Usually people observe the different manifestations of human life much too superficially, both physiologically and biologically. People do not form a picture of the whole human being in which the body, soul and spirit intertwiningly affect one another. If you wish to teach and educate children as they need, you must form such a picture.

Now those who, strengthened by spiritual scientific methods, observe the developing child will find an important developmental juncture at approximately the time of the change of teeth, around six or seven years of age. There is an oft-quoted saying that nature makes no leaps. To a certain degree, this is quite correct. However, all such views are basically one-sided. You can see their correctness only if you recognize their one-sidedness, for nature continuously makes leaps. Think about a growing plant, to name only one example. Fine. You can use this saying, nature makes no leaps. However, in the sense of Goethe's law of metamorphosis, we must say that, despite the fact that the green leaf is the same as the colorful flower petal, nature does make a leap from the leaf to the colorful petal, and yet another leap from the petal to the stamen, and another quite special leap to the fruit. We do not get along well in life if we abstractly adopt the point of view that nature, or life in general, does not make leaps. And this is particularly true with people. Human life flows along without leaps, but in this other sense, there are such leaps everywhere.

Around the age of six or seven there is a particularly important turning point that has far-reaching consequences for human structure and function. Modern physiology does not yet have a correct picture of this. Something also occurs in people in the spirit-soul realm. Until this time, human beings are fundamentally *imitative* beings. The constitution of their body and soul is such that they totally devote themselves to their surroundings. They feel their way into the surroundings. They develop themselves from the center of their will so that they mold the force lines and force rays of their will exactly to what occurs in their surroundings. More important than everything that we can bring to the child through reprimanding words, through preaching in this stage, is the way in which we ourselves behave in the presence of the child. Since the intangibles of life act much more strongly than what we can clearly observe on the surface, we must say that what the child imitates does not depend only upon the observable behavior of people. In every tone of speech, in every gesture that we as teachers use in the presence of the child during this stage, lies something to which the child adapts itself. As human beings we are much more than we know by the external reflection of our thoughts. In life we pay little attention to how we move a hand, but the way we move a hand is the faithful reflection of the whole state of our souls, the whole reflection of our inner mood. As adults with developed soul lives we pay little attention to the connection between the way we step forward with our legs, the way we gesture with our hands, the expressions on our faces, and the will and feeling impulses that lie in our souls. The child, however, lives into these intangibles. We do not exaggerate when we say that those in the young child's surroundings who inwardly strive to be good, to be moral, who in their thinking and feeling consciously intend to do the child no wrong, even in what is not spoken—such people affect the child in the strongest possible manner through the intangibles of life.

In this connection we must pay attention to what, if I may express myself so, actually lies between the lines of life. In that we slowly find ourselves caught in the web of a more materialistic life, particularly in relation to the intimacies of existence, we become accustomed to paying relatively little attention to such things. Only when we value such things again will a certain impulse enter pedagogy, an impulse particularly necessary in a time that refers to itself as social, as a socially minded period.

You see, people cannot correctly value certain experiences if they do not take into account observations of the spirit-soul nature that is the foundation of human beings. I am speaking to you about everyday events. A despairing father comes, for example, and says, "What shall I do? My child has stolen something!" We can, of course, understand how a father can despair about such things. But, now we attempt to understand the situation better. We can say, "Yes, but what were the complete circumstances?" The child simply took some money from the drawer. What did the child do with the money? The child bought something for a friend, candy, for instance. So, the child did not steal for selfish reasons. Thus, we might possibly say the child did not steal at all. There can be no talk about the child having stolen. Every day the child has seen that Mother goes to the drawer and takes money out. The child has seen that as something normal and has only imitated. This is something that has resulted from the forces that are the most important at this stage, imitation and mimicking. If you direct the child properly in this sense, if you know how to properly direct the child's attention, then this attention will be brought to all sorts of things that will have an important influence at this stage.

We must be quite conscious that reprimands and preaching at this stage do not help. Only what affects the will can help. This human characteristic exists until the moment when the remarkable physiological conclusion of childhood occurs, when "hardening" makes its final push and the permanent teeth crystallize out of the human organism. It is extremely interesting to use spiritual scientific methods to look at what lies at the basis of the developing organism, what forms the conclusion, the change of teeth. However, it is more important to follow what I have just described, the parallel spirit-soul development that arises completely from imitation.

Around the age of seven, a clear change in the spirit-soul constitution of the child begins. We could say that at this age the capacity to react to something quite differently than before emerges. Previously, the child's eye was intent upon imitating, the child's ear was intent upon imitating. Now the child begins to concentrate upon what adults radiate as opinion, as points of view. The child transforms its desire to imitate into devotion to *authority*. I know how unpleasant it is for many modern people when we make authority an important factor in education. However, if we wish to represent the facts openly and seriously, programs and slogans cannot direct us. Only empirical facts, only experience can be our guides. We need to see what it means when children have been guided by a teacher they can look up to because this teacher is a natural authority for them. That the developing human can take something into its thoughts, can live into something, because the respected adult has these thoughts and feelings, because there is a "growing together" between the developing being and the adult being, is of great importance in the development of the child. You can know what it means for the whole later life of the child only when you (I want to say this explicitly) have had the luck of having been able to devote yourself to a natural authority in the time between the transformation at around six or seven years of age and the last great transformation around the time of puberty, at about fourteen or fifteen years of age.

The main thing is not to become mired in such abstractions, but instead to enter into this very important stage of life that begins around the age of six or seven years and concludes with puberty. At this age the child, having been properly raised or spoiled through imitation, is turned over to the school by the parents. The most important things for the child's life occur in this period. This is quite true if we keep in mind that not only each year, but each month, the teacher must carefully discover the real essence of developing children. This discovery must be not only general, but as far as possible in large classes, the teacher should also carefully consider each individual child. After the child enters school, we see the residual effects of the desire to imitate alongside the beginning devotion to authority until around the age of nine (these things are all only approximate, of course). If we can properly observe the interaction of these two basic forces in the growing child, then the living result of this observation forms the proper basis not only for the teaching method, but also for the curriculum.

Excuse me if I interject a personal remark, but I encountered this very question when the Waldorf School was formed this year. Through the understanding accommodation of our friend Emil Molt and the Waldorf-Astoria firm in Stuttgart, we were able to bring a complete unified elementary school to life. We were able to bring to life a school that, in its teaching methods and in the ordering of its curriculum, is to result entirely from what the science of the spirit can say about education. In September of this year it was my pleasure to hold a seminar for the faculty I assembled for this school. All of these questions came to me in a form very fitting to our times. What I want to talk to you about now is essentially an extract of everything given to the faculty during that seminar. These teachers are to guide this truly unified elementary school according to the needs of spiritual science and contemporary society.[1]

We concerned ourselves not only with teaching methods, but particularly with creating the curriculum and teaching goals from a living observation of growing children. If we look at the growing child, we will find that after the age of six or seven much still comes from that particular kind of will that alone makes the child's desire to imitate possible to the degree I described previously. It is the will that forms the basis of this desire to imitate, not the intellect. In principle, the intellect develops from the will much later. That intimate bond between one human being, the adult teacher, and another human being, the growing child, is expressed in a relationship between will and will. Thus, we can best reach the child in these first elementary school years when we are able to properly affect the will.

How can we best affect the will? We cannot affect the will if during these years we emphasize outer appearances too strongly, if we turn the child's attention too strongly to material life. It turns out that we come particularly close to the will if in these first years we allow education to be permeated by a certain aesthetic artistry. We can really begin from this aesthetic artistry. We cannot, for example, begin with that teaching of reading and writing that does not arise from the proper connection between what we teach and the powers that come from the core of the child's soul. The letters and characters used in reading and writing consist of something quite removed from life. You need only look back at earlier characters (not those of

---

1. Translators' note: The needs of society are to be understood as both the requirements of the Department of Education and the inherent needs of a more humanly formed social organization.

primitive peoples, but, for example, those of the highly developed Egyptian culture) to see that writing was still quite artistically formed. In the course of time, this has been lost. Our characters have become conventions. On the other hand, we can go back to the direct primary relationship that people once had to what has become writing. In other words, instead of giving abstract instruction in writing, we can begin to teach writing through drawing. We should not, however, teach through just any drawings, but through the real artistic feeling in people that we can later transform into artistically formed abstract characters for the growing child. Thus, you would begin with a kind of "written drawing" or "drawn writing," and extend that by bringing the child true elements of the visual arts of painting and sculpture.

Psychologists who are genuinely concerned with the life of the soul know that what we bring to the child in this way does not reach simply the head, it reaches the whole person. What is of an intellectual color, what we permeate only with intellect, and particularly with convention, like the normal letters of reading and writing, reaches only the head. If we surround the instruction of these things with an artistic element, then we reach the whole person. Thus, a future pedagogy will attempt first to derive the intellectual element and the illustrative material from the artistic.

We can best take into account the interaction of the principles of authority and imitation if we approach the child artistically. Something of the imitative lies in the artistic. There is also something in the artistic that goes directly from subjective person to subjective person. What should act artistically must go through the subjectivity of people. As people with our own inner essence, we face the child quite differently when what we are to bring acquires an artistic form. In that way, we first pour our substance into what must naturally appear as authority. This enables us not to appear as a simple copy of conventional culture and the like, but humanly brings us closer to the child. Under the influence of this artistic education, the child will live into a recognition of the authority of the teacher as a matter of course.

At the same time, this indicates that spirit must prevail since we can teach in this way only when we allow what we have to convey to be permeated by spirit. This indicates that spirit must prevail in the entire manner of instruction, that we must live in what we have to convey. Here again I come to something that belongs to the intangibles of teaching life. People so easily believe that when they face the child they appear as the knowing, superior person before the simple, naive child. This can have very important consequences for teaching. I will show this with a specific example I have used in another connection in my lectures. Suppose I want to convey the concept of the immortality of the soul to a child. Conforming myself to the child's mood of soul, I give the example by presenting a picture. I describe a cocoon and a butterfly creeping from it in a very pictorial way. Now, I make clear to the child, "In the same way that the butterfly rests in this cocoon, invisible to the eye, your immortal soul rests in your body. Just as the butterfly leaves the cocoon, in the same way, when you go through the gates of death, your immortal soul leaves your body and rises to a world that is just as different as the butterfly's."

Well, we can do that, of course. We think out such a picture with our intellect. However, when we bring this to the child, as "reasonable" people we do not easily believe it ourselves. This affects everything in teaching. One of the intangibles of education is that, through unknown forces working between the soul of the child and the soul of the teacher, the child accepts only what I, myself, believe.

Spiritual science guides us so that the picture I just described is not simply a clever intellectual creation. We can recognize that the divine powers of creation put this picture into nature. It is there not to symbolize arbitrarily the immortality of the soul in people, but because at a lower level the same thing occurs that occurs when the immortal soul leaves the body. We can bring ourselves to believe in the direct content of this picture as much as we want, or better, as much as we should want the child to believe it. When the powers of belief prevail in the soul of the teacher, then the teacher affects the child properly. Then the effectiveness of authority does not have a disadvantage, but instead becomes a major, an important, advantage.

When we mention such things, we must always note that human life is a whole. What we plant into the human life of a child often first appears after many, many years as a fitness for life, or as a conviction in life. We take so little note of this because it emerges transformed. Let us assume we succeed in arousing a quite necessary feeling capacity in a child, namely the ability to honor. Let us assume we succeed in developing in the child a feeling for what we can honor as divine in the world, a feeling of awe. Those who have learned to see life's connections know that this feeling of awe later reappears transformed, metamorphosed. We need only recognize it again in its transformed appearance as an inner soul force that can affect other people in a healthy, in a blessed, manner. Adults who have not learned to pray as children will not have the powers of soul that can convey to children or younger people a blessing in their reprimands or facial expressions. What we received as the effect of grace during childhood transforms itself through various, largely unnoticed, phases. In the more mature stages of life it becomes something that can give forth blessing.

All kinds of forces transform themselves in this way. If we do not pay attention to these connections, if, in the art of teaching, we do not bring out the whole, wide, spiritually enlightened view of life, then education will not achieve what it should achieve. Namely, it will not be able to work *with* human developmental forces, but will work *against* them.

When people have reached approximately nine years of age, they enter a new stage that is not quite so clearly marked as the one around the age of seven years. It is, however, still quite clear. The aftereffects of the desire to imitate slowly subside, and something occurs in the growing child that, if we want to see it, can be quite closely observed. Children enter into a specific relationship to their own I. Of course, what we could call the soul relationship to the I occurs much earlier. It occurs in each person's life at the earliest moment he or she can remember. This is approximately the time when the child goes from saying, "Johnny wants this," "Mary wants this," to saying "I want this." Later, people remember back to this moment. Earlier events normally completely disappear from memory. This is when the ensouled I enters the human being. However, it has not completely entered spiritually. We see what enters the human soul constitution spiritually as the experiencing of the I that occurs in the child approximately between nine and ten years of age. People who are observers of the soul have at times mentioned this important moment in human life. Jean Paul once so beautifully said that he could remember it quite exactly. As a young boy, he was standing before a barn in the courtyard of his parents' home, so clearly could he recall it. There, the consciousness of his I awoke in him. He would never forget, so he told, how he looked through the veil at the holy of holies of the human soul.

Such a change occurs around the age of nine, in one case clearly, in another case less clearly. This moment is extremely important for the teacher. If you have previously been able to arouse in the growing child feelings tending in those directions of the will called religious or moral that you can bring forth through all your teaching, then you need only be a good observer of children to allow your authority to be effective when this stage appears. When you can observe that what you have previously prepared in the way of religious sensitivities is solidly in place and comes alive, you can meet the child with your authority.

This is the time that determines whether people can honestly and truly look from their innermost depths to something that divinely courses through the spirit and soul of the world and human life. At this point, those who can place themselves into human life through a spiritual point of view will, as teachers, be intuitively led to find the right words and the right behavior. In truth, education is something artistic. We must approach children not with a standardized pedagogy, but with an artistic pedagogy. In the same way that artists must be in control of their materials, must understand them exactly and intimately, those who work from the spiritual point of view must know the symptoms that arise around the age of nine. This is the time when people deepen their inner consciousness so that their I-consciousness becomes spiritual, whereas previously it was soulful. Then the teacher will be able to change to an objective observation of things, whereas previously the child required a connection to human subjectivity. You will know, when you can correctly judge this moment, that prior to this you should, for example, speak to children about scientific things, about things that occur in nature, by clothing them in tales, in fables, in parables. You will know that all natural objects are to be treated as having, in a sense, human characteristics. In short, you will know that you do not separate people from their natural surroundings. At that moment around the age of nine when the I awakens, human beings separate themselves from the natural environment and become mature enough to objectively compare the relationships of natural occurrences. Thus, we should not begin to objectively describe nature before this moment in the child's life. It is more important that we develop a sense, a spiritual instinct, for this important change.

Another such change occurs around eleven or twelve years of age. While the child is still completely under the influence of authority, something begins to shine into life that is fully formed only after sexual maturity. The child's developing capacity to judge begins to shine in at this time. Thus, as teachers we work so that we appeal to the child's capacity for judgment, and we allow the principle of authority to recede into the background. After about twelve years of age, the child's developing capacity for judgment already plays a role. If we correctly see the changing condition of the child's soul constitution, then we can also see that the child develops new interests. The child previously had the greatest interest, for example, in what we (of course, in a manner understandable to a child) brought in describing natural sciences. Only after this change, around eleven or twelve years of age, does this interest (I understand exactly the importance of what I say) develop into a true possibility of understanding physical phenomena, of understanding even the simplest physical concepts.

There can be no real pedagogical art without the observation of these basic underlying rhythms of human life. This art of education requires that we fit it exactly to what develops in a human being. We should derive what we call the curriculum and educational goals from that. What we teach and how we teach should flow from an understanding of human beings. However, we cannot gain this understanding of human beings if we are not able to turn our view of the world to seeing the spiritual that forms the basis of sensible facts. Then it will become clear to us that the intangibles that I have already mentioned really play a role, particularly in the pedagogical art.

Today, where our pedagogical art has developed more from the underlying scientific point of view, we place much value

upon so-called visual aids (this is the case, although we are seldom conscious of it).[2] I would ask you not to understand the
things I say as though I want to be polemic, as though I want
to preach or derogatorily criticize. This is not at all the case. I
only wish to characterize the role that the science of the spirit
can have in the formation of a pedagogical art. That we emphasize visual aids beyond their bounds is only a result of the common way of thinking that has developed from a scientific point
of view, from scientific methods. However (I will say this
expressly), regardless of how justified it is to present illustrative
materials at the proper time and with the proper subjects, it is
just as important to ask if everything we should convey to the
child can be conveyed by demonstration. We must ask if there
are no other ways in which we can bring things from the soul
of the teacher to the soul of the child. We must certainly mention that there are other ways. I have, in fact, mentioned the
all-encompassing principle of authority that is active from the
change of teeth until puberty. The child accepts the teacher's
opinion and feeling because they live in the teacher. There
must be something in the way the teacher meets the child that
acts as an intangible. There must be something that really flows
from an all-encompassing understanding of life and from the
interest in an all-encompassing understanding of life. I have
characterized it by saying that what we impart to children often
reveals itself in a metamorphosed form only in the adult, or
even in old age.

For example, there is one thing people often do not observe
because it goes beyond the boundaries of visual aids. You can
reduce what you visually present the child down to the level the
child can comprehend. You can reduce it to only what the child
can comprehend, or at least what you believe the child can

---

2. See note, p. 87.

comprehend. Those who carry this to an extreme do not notice an important rule of life, namely, that it is a source of power and strength in life if you can reach a point, for example at the age of thirty-five, when you say to yourself that as a child you learned something once from your teacher, from the person who educated you. You took it into your memory and you remembered it. Why did you remember it? Because you loved the teacher as an authority, because the essence of the teacher so stood before you that it was clear to you when that teacher truly believed something, you must learn it. This is something you did instinctively. Now you have realized something, now that you are mature. You understand it in the way I have described it —"I learned something that I learned because of a love for an authority. Now the strength of maturity arises through which I can recall it again, and I can recognize it in a new sense. Only now do I understand it."

Those who laugh at such a source of strength have no interest in real human life, they do not know that human life is a unity, that everything is connected. Thus, they cannot value what it means to go beyond normal visual aids, which are completely justifiable within their boundaries. Such people cannot value the need for their teaching to sink deeply into the child's soul so that at each new level of maturity it will always return. Why do we meet so many inwardly broken people these days? Why do our hearts bleed when we look at the broad areas in need of such tremendous undertakings, while people nonetheless wander around aimlessly? Because no one has attended to developing in growing children those capacities that later in life become a pillar of strength to enable them really to enter into life.

These are the things that we must thoroughly consider when we change from simple conventional pedagogical science to a true art of education. In order for pedagogy to be general for humanity, teachers must practice it as an individual and personal art. We must have insight into certain inner connections if we want to understand clearly what people often say instinctively but without clear understanding. Today, with some justification, people demand that we should not only educate the intellect. They say it is not so important that growing children receive knowledge or understanding. What is important is that they become industrious people, that the element of will be formed, that real dexterity be developed, and so forth. Certainly, such demands are quite justifiable. What we need to realize though is that we cannot meet such demands with general pedagogical phrases or standards; we can only meet them when we really enter into the concrete details of human developmental stages. We must know that it is the artistic aesthetic factor that fires the will, and we must be able to bring this artistic aesthetic factor to the will. We must not simply seek an external gateway to the will. That is what we would seek if we sought out people only through physiology and biology. That is what we would seek if we were not to seek them through the spiritual element that expresses itself in their being and expresses itself distinctly, particularly in childhood. There is much to be ensouled, to be spiritualized.

In our Waldorf School in Stuttgart, we have attempted for the first time to create something from what is usually based only upon the physiological, at least in its inner strength and its methods. Namely, we have attempted to transform gymnastics into the art of eurythmy. Almost every Saturday and Sunday in Dornach you can see a eurythmy performance. Eurythmy is an art form in which we use the human organism, with its possibilities for inner movement, as an instrument. What you see as an art form also has the possibility of ensouling and spiritualizing human movements that otherwise occur only in gymnastics.

Thus, people not only do what may affect this or that muscle, they also do what naturally flows from this or that feeling of the soul into the movement of the muscles, into the movement of the limbs.

Because it is based upon a spiritual scientific vitalization of life, we are convinced eurythmy will be significant for both pedagogy and healing. We are seeking the necessary healthy relationship between inner experiencing, feeling and expression of soul, and what we can develop in people as movement. We seek to develop these natural connections. We seek through the recognition of the ensouled and spiritualized human being what people usually seek only through physiology or other external facts. We can also affect the will not only when we apply the most common of arts to the principles of teaching in the early elementary school years. We can equally affect the will in a very special way when we allow soul-spirituality to permeate something also thought to cultivate the will, namely, gymnastics. However, we must recognize soul-spirituality in its concrete possibility of effectiveness, in its concrete form.

Thus, we must recognize the connections between two capacities of the human soul. Modern psychology cannot see this because it is not permeated by spiritual science. If we can look objectively at that important moment that I have described as occurring around nine years of age, we will see, on the one hand, that something important happens that is connected with the feeling capacity, the feeling life of the child. People look inwardly. Quite different feeling nuances occur. In a certain sense, the inner life of the soul becomes more independent from external nature in its feeling nuances. On the other hand, something else occurs that we can see only through a truly intimate observation of the soul. Namely, we learn because we still have what we might call an organically developed memory. Jean Paul noticed this and expressed it brilliantly when he said that we certainly learn more in the first three years of our life than in three years at the university. This is so because memory still works organically. We certainly learn more for living. However, around the age of nine a particular relationship forms between the life of feeling and the life of memory that plays more into conscious life.

We need only to see such things. If we cannot see them, then we think they are not there. If you can really see this intimate relationship between the life of feeling and memory, then you will find, if you pay attention, the proper standpoint from which to appeal to memory in your teaching. You should not appeal to memory any differently than you appeal to feeling. You will find the proper nuances, particularly for teaching history, for everything you have to say about history, if you know that you must permeate your presentation of what you want the children to remember with something that plays into their independent feelings. You will also be able to properly order the teaching of history in the curriculum if you know these connections. In this way, you can also gain a proper point of view about what the children should generally remember. You will be able to affect the feeling to the same extent you intend to affect the memory, in the same way you previously affected the will through artistic activity. Slowly, you will gain the possibility, following this stage of life, of allowing will and feeling to affect the intellect. If, in education, we do not develop the intellect in the proper way out of will and feeling, then we work in a manner opposing human developmental forces, rather than supporting them.

You can see that this whole lecture revolves around the relationship of spiritual science to pedagogical art, and how important it is to use spiritual science to provide a true understanding of human beings. In this way we obtain something from spiritual science that enters our will in the same way that artistic talents enter the human will. In this way we can remove ourselves from a pedagogy that is simply a science of convention, that always tells us to teach in this or that manner, according to some rules. We can transplant into the essence of our humanity what we must have in our will, the spiritual permeation of the will, so that from our will we can affect the developmental capacities of the growing child. In this manner, a truly effective understanding of human beings should support education in the spiritual scientific sense. The developing human thus becomes a divine riddle for us, a divine riddle that we wish to solve at every hour. If, with our art of teaching, we so place ourselves in the service of humanity, then we serve this life from our great interest in life.

Here at the conclusion, I wish to mention again the standpoint from which I began. Teachers work with people at that stage of life when we are to implant all the possibilities of life into human nature and, at the same time, to bring them forth from human nature. Then they can play a role in the whole remainder of human life and existence. For this reason we can say there is no area of life that should not, in some way or another, affect the teacher. However, only those who learn to understand life from a spiritual standpoint really understand life. To use Goethe's expression, only those who can form life spiritually will be able to form life at all. It seems to me that the most necessary thing to achieve now is the shaping of life through a pedagogy practiced more and more in conformity with the spirit. Allow me to emphasize again that what I have said today was not said to be critical, to preach. I said it because, in my modest opinion, the science of the spirit and the understanding that can be gained through it, particularly about the essence of humanity, and thus about the essence of the growing child, can serve the art of education, can provide new sources of strength for the pedagogical art.

This is the goal of spiritual science. It does not desire to be something foreign and distant from this world. It desires to be a leaven that can permeate all the capacities and tasks of life. It is with this attitude that I attempt to speak from spiritual science about the various areas of life and attempt to affect them. Also, do not attribute to arrogance what I have said today about the relationship of spiritual science to pedagogy. Rather, attribute it to an attitude rooted in the conviction that, particularly now, we must learn much about the spirit if we are to be spiritually effective in life. Attribute it to an attitude that desires to work in an honest and upright manner in the differing areas of life, that wishes to work in the most magnificent, the most noble, the most important area of life—in the teaching and shaping of human beings.

Discussion Following the Lecture

W: The speaker says that he listened to Dr. Steiner's explanation concerning pedagogy with great interest and that the same could be extended to art. He mentions Ferdinand Hodler's words that what unites people is stronger than what divides them. He then continues—

What unites us all is just that spirituality of which Dr. Steiner has spoken. Modern art also seeks this spirituality again and will find it in spite of all opposition.

I would like to mention something else. We can follow the development of children through their pictures. We often see pictures that children have painted. These pictures tell us something, if we can understand them. I will relate an experience that I, as an art teacher, have had in teaching.

I had a class draw pictures of witches. Each child expressed in the picture of the witch the bad characteristic that he or she also had. Afterward, I discussed this with the class teacher, and he told me that what I saw in the pictures was completely correct. My judgment, based upon the pictures, was completely correct.

Now a short remark concerning the way we can view modern art, the way we must view it. I can show you by means of an example. In front of us we have a blackboard. I can view this blackboard with my intellect, which tells me that this blackboard has four corners with two pairs of parallel sides and a surface that is dark and somber. My feelings tell me something else. My feelings tell me that this black, hard angular form gives me the impression of something heavy, dark, harsh, disturbing. What I first think of in seeing this blackboard, what first comes to mind, is perhaps a coffin.

It is in this way that we must understand modern pictures, no longer through reasoning, but through feeling. What do I feel in this picture, and what thoughts come to mind? We must teach children not so much to see what is externally there, but more to feel.

X: I find myself speaking now due to an inner need. In particular, I wish to express my heartfelt thanks to the lecturer for his beautiful words and for the pictures, ideas and thoughts that he unrolled before our eyes. His words have affected me extremely positively because they come from ideas with which I have concerned myself time and again for many years.

I did not know what "spiritual science" meant. Now I see quite clearly that a close connection exists between spiritual science and pedagogy. This is now my complete conviction. His words have also quite positively affected me since he demonstrated a certain development throughout the complete presentation, the development we see in the Herbart-Ziller school to which the lecturer also made reference.

The lecturer also referred to certain stages of development in children, and this causes me to make a short remark.

He has described stages in such a way that I am convinced such stages really exist. We find that Herbart also defined such stages. Already in 1804 Herbart showed, in a very interesting work concerning aesthetic form in education, what should be, what must be really important in education. From this he created the theory of stages, which Ziller carried further. These stages were to a certain degree plausibly described by Vogt in Vienna.

However, reading about all these stages had still not convinced me of their reality, of their existence, as the lecturer, Dr. Steiner, did in speaking today. For that I wish to express particular thanks.

Now one thing more. You have certainly felt that everything depends upon *one* thing, upon something that surely must lie heavily upon our souls, including my own. Everything depends upon the *personality* of the teacher. This comes out quite clearly throughout the whole lecture, with warmth, depth and responsibility. Time and again it made me particularly happy that Dr. Steiner emphasized this with complete insight and certainty. Thus, he has also shown us what a great task and responsibility we have if we wish to continue in our profession as teachers. I am generally in complete agreement with all the pictures of life he has presented. You have spoken from what I myself have experienced, thought and felt for decades. I wish to again express my most heartfelt thanks to the lecturer for his remarks.

Y: The first speaker has already expressed to a large extent what I wanted to say about how we should live into the child through art.

Now, I would like to say something somewhat critical. Dr. Steiner said that we should replace gymnastics as we now have it in the school with eurythmy. I have seen some of the eurythmy performances and understand their intent. However, I do not believe that we may use eurythmy alone in the school. What does eurythmy develop? I think that all these dancing movements ignore the human upper body, the formation of muscles. However, it is precisely this that is important to working people, and most of our elementary school students will become working people. Through eurythmy we will produce undeveloped, weak muscles, weak chest muscles, weak back muscles. The leg muscles will be strongly developed, but not those of the upper arms. They will be undeveloped and weak. We see just this weakness already today in so-called girls gymnastics, where the tendency is already to lay too much value upon dancing. Where the strength of the upper arms is demanded, these muscles fail. These girls cannot even do the simplest exercises requiring support of the arms. However, this is much less important to girls than it is to boys in their later work. If we take eurythmy and leave aside physiological gymnastics—the parallel bars, the high bar, rope climbing—then I fear that the strength people need in their work may suffer. What I wish to say is that we can teach eurythmy, and the children will receive an aesthetic training, but it should not be eurythmy alone. What pleased me at the performances in Dornach was the beautiful play of lines, the harmony of the movements, the artistic, the aesthetic. However, I would doubt that these eurythmy exercises can really play a part in making the body suitable for working. I would like to hear a further explanation if Dr. Steiner desires to have only eurythmy exercise, if he desires to deny school gymnastics, based in physiological facts, its rightful place. If we were to deny those physical exercises based upon an understanding of the human body their rightful place, then I would be unable to agree completely with the introduction of eurythmy into the schools.

Dr. Steiner: I would first like to say a few words concerning the last point so that misunderstandings do not arise. Perhaps I did not make this clear enough in the lecture, since I could only briefly discuss the subject. When we present eurythmy in Dornach, we do this, of course, as an *artistic* activity, in that we emphasize just what you referred to as being pleasant. In that we emphasize what can be pleasant, in Dornach we must, of course, present those things meant more for viewing, for an artistic presentation. In the lecture I wanted to indicate more that in viewing eurythmy people would recognize that what they normally think of as simply physiological (this is somewhat radically said, since gymnastics is not thought of as only physiological), what is primarily thought of as only physiological, can be spiritualized and ensouled. If you include eurythmy in the curriculum (when I introduce a eurythmy performance, I normally mention that eurythmy is only in its beginning stages), and if today it seems one-sided in that it particularly develops certain limbs, this will disappear when we develop eurythmy further. I need to mention this so as not to leave the impression that I believe we should drop gymnastics.

You see, in the Waldorf School in Stuttgart, we have a period of normal gymnastics and a period of eurythmy, consisting of more than you see in an artistic presentation. Thus, we take into account the requirements that you justifiably presented.

What is important to me is that along with the physical, the physiological that forms the basis of gymnastics, we add the spirit and soul, so that both things are present. Just as people themselves consist of a totality in the interaction of body, soul and spirit, what is truly the soul, recognizable for itself, also works in the movements that people carry out in gymnastics and such. We are not at all concerned with eliminating gymnastics. Quite the opposite. It is my desire that gymnastics be enriched with eurythmy. We should not eliminate one single exercise on the parallel bars or high bar. We should leave out nothing in gymnastics. However, what eurythmy attempts is that instead of asking how we can handle this or that muscle from the physiological point of view, the question becomes how does a soul impulse work? In other words, alongside what already exists, we add something else. I do not at all wish to criticize what already exists, but rather to describe briefly what spiritual science fosters in the way of permeating things with spirit and soul. I agree with your objection, but it is my desire to show that bringing the soul element into gymnastics can originate from the science of the spirit.

Z: Mr. Z describes how the principle that Dr. Steiner has developed would be extremely educational and fruitful for the school.

If people were to consider how schools now handle things, they would have to say that this does not correspond to the stages described by Dr. Steiner. Goethe once said that children must go through the cultures of humanity to develop their feeling life. If we want to connect with these valuable words from Goethe and make them fruitful, we should have methods that are completely contrary to the ideas we have used for years. The second thing I would like to mention is that in drawing, we always begin with lines and figures. If we look at the drawings of the cave dwellers, we must realize that they did not have any instruction in drawing at all. I think that we can learn a great deal for teaching drawing to our children from the first drawings and paintings of those primitive people. Regarding singing, we now begin with the scale, as if that was the natural basis for singing in school. However, if we study the history of music, we will immediately see that the scale is an abstraction to which humanity has come only over many centuries. The primary thing in music is the triad, the chord in general. Thus, our singing instruction should much more properly begin with chords and only later come to scales. For other subjects, such as geography and history, I think we should pay much more attention to how primitive people first obtained this (I dare not say science), this knowledge. We could then continue in the same way. For example, we could present geography beginning with interesting drawings of the trips of discovery to the New World, and so forth. Then the children would show much, much more interest because we would have enlivened the subject instead of presenting them with the finished results as is done today in the dry textbooks and through the dry instructions—"ob-structions."[3]

Dr. Steiner: It is now much too late for me to attempt to give any real concluding remarks. I am touched with a deep sense of satisfaction that what has come forth from the various speakers in the discussion was extremely interesting, and fell very naturally into what I intended in the lecture. It's true, isn't it, that you can comprehend in what, for example, you can see in Dornach, in what we present in the various artistic activities in Dornach, that something is given that reflects the fundamental conviction of spiritual science.

Now the gentleman who just spoke so beautifully about how we can educate for artistic feeling rather than mere viewing, would see that spiritual science artistically attempts to do justice to such things. He would see that in Dornach we attempt to paint purely from color, so that people also feel the inner content of the color, of the colored surface, and that what occurs as a line results from the colored area. In this

---

3. Translators' note: This is a word play in German: *Leitfäden—Leidfäden*

regard, what is substantial in spiritual science can work to enliven much of what it touches today. The remarks about the Herbartian pedagogy were extremely interesting to me, since in both a positive and negative sense we can learn much from Herbart. This is particularly true when we see that in the Herbartian psychology, in spite of a methodical striving toward the formation of the will, intellectualism has played a major role. You must struggle past much in Herbartian pedagogy in order to come to the principles that result from my explanation today.

Regarding the last speaker, I agree with almost everything. He could convince himself that the kind of education he demands, in all its details, belongs to the principle direction of our Waldorf School, particularly concerning the methods of teaching drawing, music and geography. We have put forth much effort, particularly in these three areas, to bring into a practical form just what the speaker imagines. For instance, in the faculty seminar we did a practice presentation about the Mississippi Valley. I think the way we prepared this presentation of a living, vivid geography lesson that does not come from some theory or intellectuality, but from human experience, would have been very satisfactory to the speaker. In place of a closing word, I therefore only wish to say that I am extremely satisfied that so many people gave such encouraging and important additions to the lecture.

The Pedagogical Objective
of the Waldorf School in Stuttgart

An Essay from *The Social Future,* February 1920

ANYONE WHO PREPARES for the teaching profession at a modern school of education certainly takes good principles about the educational system and the art of teaching into life. Many to whom this task falls undoubtedly have the good will to actually use these principles. Nevertheless, there is a far-reaching feeling of discontent in this profession. New, or apparently new, objectives continually emerge. We create new institutions which are supposed to meet the demands of human nature and social life in a better way than those which preceded them. It would be unfair not to acknowledge that for more than a century the caretakers of pedagogy and didactics have been the noblest people, borne by high idealism. Their legacy provides the new teacher with a rich treasure of pedagogical wisdom and inspiring practical advice.

Unquestionably, the ideas that are available from leading educators, if they are adhered to, could remedy every shortcoming of education and teaching. The cause of such discontent cannot be the absence of a carefully cultivated pedagogy. It also cannot come from a lack of good will on the part of those who are active in education and teaching. This discontent is, however, not unfounded. The life experiences of every impartial person prove that.

Those participating in the establishment of the Waldorf School in Stuttgart are filled with such feelings. Emil Molt, the founder of the school, and the author (who has been permitted to give direction in the method of teaching and instruction, and who will continue to provide guidance in this area) wish to solve a pedagogical and social problem with this school.

In attempting to solve the pedagogical problem it is important to recognize why the good principles of education that are so widely available do not lead to satisfying results. For example, people generally acknowledge that we must observe the child's developing personality to derive the basic ideas of teaching and education. In all kinds of ways people assert that this point of view is correct.

Today, however, difficult obstacles must be overcome in taking this point of view. We need a spiritual understanding that really unlocks the nature of humanity to make a true practice effective. The point of view that dominates modern thinking does not lead to such understanding. This point of view believes that it has a firm footing only if it can set up universally valid laws— laws that can be expressed as concrete ideas and then applied to specific cases. If people have received their training in a modern institution of education, they are accustomed to the search for such laws. Even people predestined to become educators are accustomed to thinking in these terms. However, the essence of the human soul escapes comprehension if we try to understand it through such laws. Only nature yields up these laws.

If we want to comprehend the essence of the soul, we must suffuse our mechanical understanding with artistic creativity. To comprehend the spiritual, the observer must become an artistic viewer. Now you could claim that such an understanding is not true understanding since it involves personal experience in the comprehension of things. There may be many logical preconceptions that support such a claim, but what speaks against it is that without the inclusion of personal inner experiences, of creative comprehension, we cannot recognize the spiritual. People shy away from the inclusion of personal experience because they believe that they must thereby step into the trap of arbitrary personal judgment. It is certainly possible to become arbitrary if we do not achieve inner objectivity through careful self-development.

Thus, the path is indicated for those who accept the validity of spiritual knowledge alongside the conventional knowledge of the field. The task of unlocking the essence of the soul falls to spiritual knowledge; and spiritual knowledge must be the foundation of a real art of education and instruction. An understanding of spiritual knowledge leads to an understanding of human nature that is so vibrant, that has such living ideas, that the teacher can shape them to meet the individual needs of the children. The demand to teach and educate according to the needs of the children has a practical meaning only for those teachers who can do this.

In our time, with its intellectualism and its love for abstractions, some people might attempt to refute this. Some might, for instance, object that it is quite obvious that we should interpret general ideas concerning human nature, including those concerned with modern society, for specific cases.

To guide educationally each individual child by interpreting general ideas, we must acquire, through a particular spiritual knowledge, an eye for what *cannot* be included as a specific case under a general rule—for that rule first must be understood through the specific case. Unlike the model of normal cognition, the spiritual knowledge meant here does not lead to a set of general ideas and to their utilization in specific cases. Rather it brings people to a certain condition of the soul, so that they may, through observation, experience the particular case in its individuality.

This spiritual science pursues the question of how humans develop in childhood and youth. It shows how the natural tendency of the child, during the period from birth until the change of teeth, is to develop out of a compulsion to *copy.* What the child sees, hears, etc., evokes a compulsion to do the same. Spiritual science explores in detail how this compulsion unfolds. For such investigations, we need methods that guide simple mechanical thinking into artistic observation at every opportunity. Only in this way can we examine what excites children to imitate, and how they imitate.

At the time of the change of teeth, the child's experiencing undergoes a complete reversal. The desire arises to do or think what another person perceived by the child as an authority does or thinks, if that person indicates that the deed or thought is right. Before this stage of life, imitation makes the child's own being a copy of the environment. With the entrance into this stage of life, the child does not *merely* imitate, but absorbs another being into itself with a certain degree of consciousness. However, until about nine years of age, the compulsion to imitate continues alongside the new desire to follow authority. If we begin with how these two main compulsions are expressed in these two successive stages of childhood, further aspects of the child's nature will reveal themselves. We get to know the living, pliant development of childhood.

What is really significant escapes those in the field of education who make their observations in the way that is right for observing both natural things and humans as creatures of nature. However, those who use a method of observation appropriate to the field of education sharpen the ability to see the specifics of a child's essence. For such people, a child is not a specific case judged according to general rules but a single question needing an answer.

Now people will object that it would not be possible in a class with many children to concentrate on each child with such depth. Without wanting to suggest that classes should be overcrowded, we must say that a teacher who possesses the kind of spiritual cognition meant here can more easily manage a large class than another teacher who does not have this cognition. This spiritual understanding reveals itself in the entire demeanor of the teacher. It will give character to each word, to everything done by the teacher. Under the guidance of the teacher, the children will become inwardly active. The teacher's general conduct will affect the children in such a way that they do not need to be forced into activity.

The appropriate curriculum and teaching methods come from knowledge of the child's development. If we understand how the desire to imitate and the need to be directed out of authority work together in the child during the first years of elementary school, we will know, for instance, how to teach writing. If we base our methods on a purely intellectual understanding, we will work against the strengths present in the child's desire to imitate. However, if we begin with drawing and gradually guide the child to writing, we will develop what strives toward development. In this way, the curriculum can come entirely from the way the child develops. Only a curriculum derived in this way works in the direction of human development. It makes people strong. All others weaken people and this weakening affects their whole lives.

Only through the kind of spiritual understanding described here can an educational principle, like the necessity of respecting the child's individuality, be used. A pedagogy that wants to put into practice what many support as a theoretically good principle must be based upon a true spiritual science. Otherwise, only those few teachers who, through fortunate circumstance, have the natural ability to form instinctively their own teaching methods can use it. The pedagogical and didactic teaching of the Waldorf School should receive its impulse from a true spiritual scientific understanding of people. I set myself the task of motivating the teachers in this direction in a seminar on spiritual scientific pedagogy and didactics that I held for them before the school opened.

This school is a first attempt at solving these briefly outlined pedagogical tasks. At the same time, Emil Molt has created an organization in the Waldorf School that corresponds to a current social demand. The school is the elementary school for the children of the Waldorf-Astoria factory employees. Children from different social classes sit next to each other, thus fully preserving the character of a unified elementary school. That is all that one person can do at first. In a broader sense, the school can solve an important future social problem only if society integrates the schools in such a way that the spirit of the Waldorf School can permeate them as far as possible under present conditions.

The above description shows that we must build all pedagogical art on a knowledge of the soul that is closely tied to the personality of the teacher. This personality must be able to freely express itself in pedagogical creativity. That, however, is possible only if the entire administration of the school system is autonomous, if practicing teachers need to deal only with other practicing teachers in administrative questions. An educator not actively teaching would be just as much out of place in the school administration as a person without artistic creativity would be in giving directions to creative artists. The nature of the pedagogical art requires that the faculty divide its time between teaching and administering the school. The spirit formed out of the attitude of all teachers united in an educating community thus comes to full effect in the administration. In this community only what comes from a recognition, an understanding, of the soul will have value.

Such a community is possible only in the Threefold Social Organism, which has a free cultural life alongside a democratically oriented state and an independent economic life. (Refer to the articles in the preceding numbers of *Soziale Zukunft* [The social future] for information concerning the nature of the Threefold Social Organism.[1]) A cultural life that receives its directives from the political bureaucracy or from the forces of economic life cannot take care of a school whose impulse derives solely from the faculty. However, a free school will prepare people for life, people who can work to their full capacity in politics and industry, because these capacities were fully developed.

Those people who do not share the opinion that the impersonal means of production or similar things shape people, but instead recognize from factual reality how people create society, will recognize the importance of a school not based on party or other such standpoints. They will recognize the importance of a school based upon what the depths of cosmic existence convey to the human community through the new generation entering the community. To recognize and develop this, however, is only possible from a spiritual point of view, as this article has tried to describe. From this point of view, the profound importance of a pedagogical practice founded upon spiritual science is apparent.

Educators will have to judge much in this pedagogical practice in a way different from that of the present. To mention only one thing, we should note that alongside ordinary gymnastics, in the Waldorf School we established a kind of eurythmy as

---

1. Translators' note: Dr. Steiner is referring to the monthly journal (i.e., not the lecture cycle published in English under the same title). Some of the articles referenced here can be found in German in GA 24, *Über die Dreigliederung des sozialen Organismus und zur Zeitlage Schriften und Aufsätze 1915-1921,* partially available in English as *The Renewal of the Social Organism,* Anthroposophic Press, 1985.

equally important. This eurythmy is a visible language. It provides exercise to the human limbs. People and groups of people move in a way that expresses a soul content, much in the same way as in speaking or music. People are inspired in their movements. Even though today gymnastics, which can work directly only on strengthening the body and, at best, can work indirectly on strengthening moral character, is prejudicially overvalued, a later time will recognize how the inspirational movement art of eurythmy develops the initiative to will while at the same time strengthening the body. It encompasses people as a whole in body, soul and spirit.

Those people who do not allow the current crisis of European civilization to pass by in a kind of soul sleep but fully experience it will see that it did not originate in institutions that simply missed their goals and that simply need improvement. Those people will look for the cause deep in human thinking, feeling and willing. They will also acknowledge that the education of the coming generation is one of the ways leading to a revitalization of our social life. They will not leave unnoticed an attempt which seeks a revitalization in pedagogical art and through which good principles and good will can come to life. The Waldorf School is not an "alternative" school like so many others founded in the belief that they will correct all the errors of one kind or another in education. It is founded on the idea that the best principles and the best will in this field can come into effect only if the teacher understands human nature. However, this understanding is not possible without developing an active interest in all of human social life. The heart thus opened to human nature accepts all human sorrow and all human joy as its own experience. Through a teacher who understands the soul, who understands people, the totality of social life affects the new generation struggling into life. People will emerge from this school fully prepared for life.

Publisher's Note Regarding Rudolf Steiner's Lectures

The lectures contained in this volume have been translated from the German edition, which is based on stenographic and other recorded texts that were in most cases never seen or revised by the lecturer. Hence, due to human errors in hearing and transcription, they may contain mistakes and faulty passages. We have made every effort to ensure that this is not the case. Some of the lectures were given to audiences more familiar with anthroposophy; these are the so-called "private" or "members" lectures. Other lectures, like the written works, were intended for the general public. The difference between these, as Rudolf Steiner indicates in his *Autobiography*, is two-fold. On the one hand, the members' lectures take for granted a background in and commitment to anthroposophy; in the public lectures this was not the case. At the same time, the members' lectures address the concerns and dilemmas of the members, while the public work speaks directly out of Steiner's own understanding of universal needs. Nevertheless, as Rudolf Steiner stresses: "Nothing was ever said that was not solely the result of my direct experience of the growing content of anthroposophy. There was never any question of concessions to the prejudices and preferences of the members. Whoever reads these privately printed lectures can take them to represent anthroposophy in the fullest sense. Thus it was possible without hesitation—when the complaints in this direction became too persistent—to depart from the custom of circulating this material 'for members only.' But it must be born in mind that faulty passages do occur in these reports not revised by myself." Earlier in the same chapter, he states: "Had I been able to correct them [the private lectures] the restriction *for members only* would have been unnecessary from the beginning."

THE FOUNDATIONS
OF WALDORF EDUCATION

THE FIRST FREE WALDORF SCHOOL opened its doors in Stuttgart, Germany, in September, 1919, under the auspices of Emil Molt, the Director of the Waldorf-Astoria Cigarette Company and a student of Rudolf Steiner's spiritual science and particularly of Steiner's call for social renewal.

It was only the previous year—amid the social chaos following the end of World War I—that Emil Molt, responding to Steiner's prognosis that truly human change would not be possible unless a sufficient number of people received an education that developed the whole human being, decided to create a school for his workers' children. Conversations with the Minister of Education and with Rudolf Steiner, in early 1919, then led rapidly to the forming of the first school.

Since that time, more than six hundred schools have opened around the globe—from Italy, France, Portugal, Spain, Holland, Belgium, Great Britain, Norway, Finland and Sweden to Russia, Georgia, Poland, Hungary, Rumania, Israel, South Africa, Australia, Brazil, Chile, Peru, Argentina, Japan etc.—making the Waldorf School Movement the largest independent school movement in the world. The United States, Canada, and Mexico alone now have more than 120 schools.

Although each Waldorf school is independent, and although there is a healthy oral tradition going back to the first Waldorf teachers and to Steiner himself, as well as a growing body of secondary literature, the true foundations of the Waldorf method and spirit remain the many lectures that Rudolf Steiner gave on the subject. For five years (1919–24), Rudolf Steiner, while simultaneously working on many other fronts, tirelessly dedicated himself to the dissemination of the idea of Waldorf education. He gave manifold lectures to teachers, parents, the general public, and even the children themselves. New schools were founded. The Movement grew.

While many of Steiner's foundational lectures have been translated and published in the past, some have never appeared in English, and many have been virtually unobtainable for years. To remedy this situation and to establish a coherent basis for Waldorf Education, Anthroposophic Press has decided to publish the complete series of Steiner lectures and writings on education in a uniform series. This series will thus constitute an authoritative foundation for work in educational renewal, for Waldorf teachers, parents, and educators generally.

. . . .

RUDOLF STEINER'S LECTURES (AND WRITINGS) ON EDUCATION

I. *Allgemeine Menschenkunde als Grundlage der Pädagogik. Pädagogischer Grundkurs,* 14 Lectures, Stuttgart, 1919 (GA 293). Previously *Study of Man. The Foundations of Human Experience* (Anthroposophic Press, 1996).

II. *Erziehungskunst Methodische-Didaktisches,* 14 Lectures, Stuttgart, 1919 (GA 294). *Practical Advice to Teachers* (Rudolf Steiner Press, 1988).

III. *Erziehungskunst,* 15 Discussions, Stuttgart, 1919 (GA 295). *Discussions with Teachers* (Anthroposophic Press, 1997).

IV. *Die Erziehungsfrage als soziale Frage,* 6 Lectures, Dornach, 1919 (GA 296). *Education as a Force for Social Change* (previously *Education as a Social Problem*) (Anthroposophic Press, 1997).

V. *Die Waldorf Schule und ihr Geist,* 6 Lectures, Stuttgart and Basel, 1919 (GA 297). *The Spirit of the Waldorf School* (Anthroposophic Press, 1995).

VI. *Rudolf Steiner in der Waldorfschule, Vorträge und Ansprachen,* Stuttgart, 1919–1924 (GA 298). *Rudolf Steiner in the Waldorf School—Lectures and Conversations* (Anthroposophic Press, 1996).

VII. *Geisteswissenschaftliche Sprachbetrachtungen,* 6 Lectures, Stuttgart, 1919 (GA 299). *The Genius of Language* (Anthroposophic Press, 1995).

VIII. *Konferenzen mit den Lehren der Freien Waldorfschule 1919–1924*, 3 Volumes (GA 300). *Conferences with Teachers* (Steiner Schools Fellowship, 1986, 1987, 1988, 1989).

IX. *Die Erneuerung der Pädagogisch-didaktischen Kunst durch Geisteswissenschaft*, 14 Lectures, Basel, 1920 (GA 301). *The Renewal of Education* (Kolisko Archive Publications for Steiner Schools Fellowship Publications, Michael Hall, Forest Row, East Sussex, UK, 1981).

X. *Menschenerkenntnis und Unterrichtsgestaltung*, 8 Lectures, Stuttgart, 1921 (GA 302). Previously *The Supplementary Course—Upper School* and *Waldorf Education for Adolescence. Education for Adolescents* (Anthroposophic Press, 1996).

XI. *Erziehung und Unterricht aus Menschenerkenntnis*, 9 Lectures, Stuttgart, 1920, 1922, 1923 (GA 302a). The first four lectures available as *Balance in Teaching* (Mercury Press, 1982); last three lectures as *Deeper Insights into Education* (Anthroposophic Press, 1988).

XII. *Die Gesunder Entwicklung des Menschenwesens,* 16 Lectures, Dornach, 1921–22 (GA 303). *Soul Economy and Waldorf Education* (Anthroposophic Press, 1986).

XIII. *Erziehungs- und Unterrichtsmethoden auf Anthroposophischer Grundlage*, 9 Public Lectures, various cities, 1921–22 (GA 304). *Waldorf Education and Anthroposophy 1* (Anthroposophic Press, 1995).

XIV. *Anthroposophische Menschenkunde und Pädagogik*, 9 Public Lectures, various cities, 1923–24 (GA 304a). *Waldorf Education and Anthroposophy 2* (Anthroposophic Press, 1996).

XV. *Die geistig-seelischen Grundkräfte der Erziehungskunst*, 12 Lectures, 1 Special Lecture, Oxford 1922 (GA 305). *The Spiritual Ground of Education* (Garber Publications, 1989).

XVI. *Die pädagogisch Praxis vom Gesichtspunkte geisteswissenschaftlicher Menschenerkenntnis*, 8 Lectures, Dornach, 1923 (GA 306). *The Child's Changing Consciousness As the Basis of Pedagogical Practice* (Anthroposophic Press, 1996).

XVII. *Gegenwärtiges Geistesleben und Erziehung,* 4 Lectures, Ilkeley, 1923 (GA 307). *A Modern Art of Education* (Rudolf Steiner Press, 1981) and *Education and Modern Spiritual Life* (Garber Publications, n.d.).

XVIII. *Die Methodik des Lehrens und die Lebensbedingungen des Erziehens*, 5 Lectures, Stuttgart, 1924 (GA 308). *The Essentials of Education* (Anthroposophic Press, 1997).

XIX. *Anthroposophische Pädagogik und ihre Voraussetzungen*, 5 Lectures, Bern, 1924 (GA 309). *The Roots of Education* (Anthroposophic Press, 1997).

XX. *Der pädagogische Wert der Menschenerkenntnis und der Kulturwert der Pädagogik,* 10 Public Lectures, Arnheim, 1924 (GA 310). *Human Values in Education* (Rudolf Steiner Press, 1971).

XXI. *Die Kunst des Erziehens aus dem Erfassen der Menschenwesenheit,* 7 Lectures, Torquay, 1924 (GA 311). *The Kingdom of Childhood* (Anthroposophic Press, 1995).

XXII. *Geisteswissenschaftliche Impulse zur Entwicklung der Physik. Erster naturwissenschaftliche Kurs: Licht, Farbe, Ton—Masse, Elektrizität, Magnetismus,* 10 Lectures, Stuttgart, 1919–20 (GA 320). *The Light Course* (Steiner Schools Fellowship,1977).

XXIII. *Geisteswissenschaftliche Impulse zur Entwicklung der Physik. Zweiter naturwissenschaftliche Kurs: die Wärme auf der Grenze positiver und negativer Materialität,* 14 Lectures, Stuttgart, 1920 (GA 321). *The Warmth Course* (Mercury Press, 1988).

XXIV. *Das Verhältnis der verschiedenen naturwissenschaftlichen Gebiete zur Astronomie. Dritter naturwissenschaftliche Kurs: Himmelskunde in Beziehung zum Menschen und zur Menschenkunde,* 18 Lectures, Stuttgart, 1921 (GA 323). Available in typescript only as "The Relation of the Diverse Branches of Natural Science to Astronomy."

XXV. *The Education of the Child and Early Lectures on Education* (A collection) (Anthroposophic Press, 1996).

XXVI. Miscellaneous.

Bibliography

Basic Works by Rudolf Steiner

Anthroposophy (A Fragment), Anthroposophic Press, Hudson, NY, 1996.

An Autobiography, Steinerbooks, Blauvelt, NY, 1977.

Christianity as Mystical Fact, Anthroposophic Press, Hudson, NY, 1997.

How to Know Higher Worlds: A Modern Path of Initiation, Anthroposophic Press, Hudson, NY, 1994.

Intuitive Thinking as a Spiritual Path: A Philosophy of Freedom, Anthroposophic Press, Hudson, NY, 1995 (previously translated as *Philosophy of Spiritual Activity*).

An Outline of Esoteric Science, Anthroposophic Press, Hudson, NY, 1997 (previous translation titled *An Outline of Occult Science*).

A Road to Self-Knowledge and The Threshold of the Spiritual World, Rudolf Steiner Press, London, 1975.

Theosophy: An Introduction to the Spiritual Processes in Human Life and in the Cosmos, Anthroposophic Press, Hudson, NY, 1994.

Books by Other Authors

Anschütz, Marieke. *Children and Their Temperaments,* Floris Books, Edinburgh, 1995.

Britz-Crecelius, Heidi. *Children at Play: Using Waldorf Principles to Foster Childhood Development,* Park Street Press, Rochester, VT, 1996.

Carlgren, Frans. *Education Towards Freedom: Rudolf Steiner Education: A Survey of the Work of Waldorf Schools Throughout the World,* Lanthorn Press, East Grinstead, England, 1993.

Childs, Gilbert. *Education and Beyond: Steiner and the Problems of Modern Society,* Floris Books, Edinburgh, 1996.

—— *Understanding Your Temperament! A Guide to the Four Temperaments,* Sophia Books, London, 1995.

Childs, Dr. Gilbert and Sylvia Childs. *Your Reincarnating Child,* Sophia Books/Rudolf Steiner Press, London, 1995.

Edmunds, L. Francis. *Renewing Education: Selected Writings on Steiner Education,* Hawthorn Press, Stroud, UK, 1992.

——*Rudolf Steiner Education: The Waldorf School,* Rudolf Steiner Press, London, 1992.

Fenner, Pamela Johnson and Karen L. Rivers, eds. *Waldorf Student Reading List,* third edition, Michaelmas Press, Amesbury, MA, 1995.

Finser, Torin M. *School as a Journey: The Eight-Year Odyssey of a Waldorf Teacher and His Class,* Anthroposophic Press, Hudson, NY, 1994.

Gabert, Erich. *Educating the Adolescent: Discipline or Freedom,* Anthroposophic Press, Hudson, NY, 1988.

Gardner, John Fentress. *Education in Search of the Spirit: Essays on American Education,* Anthroposophic Press, Hudson, NY, 1996.

——*Youth Longs to Know: Explorations of the Spirit in Education,* Anthroposophic Press, Hudson, NY, 1997.

Gatto, John Taylor. *Dumbing Us Down: The Hidden Curriculum of Compulsory Schooling,* New Society, Philadelphia, 1992.

Harwood, A. C. *The Recovery of Man in Childhood: A Study in the Educational Work of Rudolf Steiner,* The Myrin Institute of New York, New York, 1992.

Heider, Molly von. *Looking Forward: Games, rhymes and exercises to help children develop their learning abilities,* Hawthorn Press, Stroud, UK, 1995.

Heydebrand, Caroline von, *Childhood: A Study of the Growing Child,* Anthroposophic Press, Hudson, NY, 1995.

Jaffke, Freya. *Work and Play in Early Childhood,* Anthroposophic Press, Hudson, NY, 1996.

Large, Martin. *Who's Bringing Them Up? How to Break the T.V. Habit!* Hawthorn Press, Stroud, UK, 1990.

Nobel, Agnes. *Educating through Art: The Steiner School Approach,* Floris Books, Edinburgh, 1996.

Pusch, Ruth, ed. *Waldorf Schools Volume I: Kindergarten and Early Grades,* Mercury Press, Spring Valley, NY, 1993.

—— *Waldorf Schools Volume II: Upper Grades and High School,* Mercury Press, Spring Valley, NY, 1993.

Richards, M. C. *Opening Our Moral Eye,* Lindisfarne Books, Hudson, NY, 1996.

Spock, Marjorie. *Teaching as a Lively Art,* Anthroposophic Press, Hudson, NY, 1985.

Index

DURING THE LAST TWO DECADES of the nineteenth century the Austrian-born Rudolf Steiner (1861–1925) became a respected and well-published scientific, literary, and philosophical scholar, particularly known for his work on Goethe's scientific writings. After the turn of the century he began to develop his earlier philosophical principles into an approach to methodical research of psychological and spiritual phenomena.

His multifaceted genius has led to innovative and holistic approaches in medicine, science, education (Waldorf schools), special education, philosophy, religion, economics, agriculture (Biodynamic method), architecture, drama, new arts of eurythmy and speech, and other fields. In 1924 he founded the General Anthroposophical Society, which today has branches throughout the world.

. . . .

*For an informative catalog of the work of Rudolf Steiner
and other anthroposophical authors please contact*

ANTHROPOSOPHIC PRESS
3390 Route 9, Hudson, NY 12534
TEL: 518 851 2054
FAX: 518 851 2047